Men-at-Arms • 4

The Army of the German Empire 1870-88

Albert Seaton • Illustrated by Michael Youens
Series editor Martin Windrow

First published in Great Britain in 1973 by Osprey Publishing,
PO Box 883, Oxford, OX1 9PL, UK
PO Box 3985, New York, NY 10185-3985, USA
Email: info@ospreypublishing.com

Osprey Publishing, part of Bloomsbury Publishing Plc

© 1973 Osprey Publishing Ltd.

All rights reserved. Apart from any fair dealing for the purpose of private study, research, criticism or review, as permitted under the Copyright, Designs and Patents Act, 1988, no part of this publication may be reproduced, stored in a retrieval system, or transmitted in any form or by any means, electronic, electrical, chemical, mechanical, optical, photocopying, recording or otherwise, without the prior written permission of the copyright owner. Enquiries should be addressed to the Publishers.

Transferred to digital print on demand 2016.

First published 1973
5th impression 2008

Printed and bound by PrintOnDemand-Worldwide.com, Peterborough, UK.

A CIP catalogue record for this book is available from the British Library.

ISBN: 978 0 85045 150 4

Series Editor: Martin Windrow

Acknowledgements
In the preparation of the plates, illustrations and text, acknowledgement is made to Arnould's *Das Deutsche Heer* (Wandsbek-Hamburg 1891). The plates are reproduced by courtesy of the Keeper, The Library of the Victoria and Albert Museum (photographer Berkhamsted Photographic, Berkhamsted, Hertfordshire).

The Woodland Trust
Osprey Publishing are supporting the Woodland Trust, the UK's leading woodland conservation charity, by funding the dedication of trees.

www.ospreypublishing.com

The Army of the German Empire, 1870-1888

Introduction

The German Empire and the German Army owed their origins to Prussia, that is to say the Duchy of East Prussia and Mark Brandenburg which together eventually formed the Kingdom of Prussia.

The first Prussian standing army was that raised by the Electors of Brandenburg consisting of free companies of mercenaries (Landsknechte) stationed in peace in the main cities and fortresses. In war, though their numbers were increased, they proved unsatisfactory since their services could be bought by the enemy. Desertion was common and there was no means of compelling the mercenaries to undertake tasks which were not to their liking. During the Thirty Years War the Elector George William raised an army of 10,000 men for service against Sweden, but even this was largely independent of Prussia since the troops had been recruited and paid in part by the Austrian Emperor. The corps of officers was in the hands of foreign adventurers.

Frederick William, the Great Elector, succeeded his father in 1640 when the Thirty Years War was at its height. Brandenburg had been ravaged by the war and the population of Berlin stood at less than 300 inhabitants. Prussia, the cockpit of Europe, was the battleground for the major military powers, France to the west, Poland to the east, Sweden on the Baltic shore and Austria in the south. To secure his independence and safeguard what was left of his realm, the Elector was obliged to raise a national Prussian Army, the first of its kind. The noble and educated classes of society were directed to become officers, and their young sons were sent for three-year courses at the newly-founded academies. The peacetime military establishments were related to war needs so that the cadres could be rapidly increased on mobilization.

By 1688 Frederick William had created a well trained army of over 30,000 men, including thirty-six battalions of infantry, thirty-two squadrons of cuirassiers and eight of dragoons, in spite of the fact that the total Prussian population numbered no more than one and a half million. In Prussia the era of the mercenary was past.

Under his successor, Frederick III (from 1701 King Frederick I of Prussia) the army continued to expand, seeing foreign service against the French, usually as part of the imperial forces, during the War of the Spanish Succession. At the time of the death of Frederick I in 1713 it numbered just over 40,000 men.

Soldiers of the Magdeburg Hussars (Regiment No. 10)

Prussia's Greatest Warrior

Frederick's successor, Frederick William I (1713–40) was a man of peace. Yet his whole life was directed towards preparing for war. The new king was an excellent administrator for, by the most rigid of economies, he contrived to double the military establishment with no increase of military expenditure. Recruiting was put on a more regular footing, the volunteer system (which had always been augmented by crimping and the press gang) being replaced by regular conscription. Admittedly, the conscription law was neither egalitarian nor just, since there were too many exemptions on the grounds of birth or wealth, but the nobility was expected to serve voluntarily, either in the army or in the state service. And this they did readily. Provinces were divided into recruiting areas, forming the basis of the latter-day system of recruiting districts.

The Sergeant-King was obsessed with discipline, regularity and good order, with the minutiae of uniform and equipment and, in particular, with the organization and training of infantry. At his death in 1740 he bequeathed to his son Frederick II (the Great) sixty-six battalions of infantry and 114 squadrons of cavalry, in all just over 80,000 men. The cost of maintaining this army, according to the 1739 estimates, was 4,900,000 thalers out of a gross revenue of 7,400,000 thalers. The young Frederick was determined to put this excellent army to immediate use, and his seizure of Austrian Silesia gave rise to the three Silesian Wars between Prussia and Austria. At one time Frederick, whose Prussian subjects numbered no more than four and a half million, was at war against Austria, Russia, France, Poland-Saxony and Sweden; his only ally was Great Britain and he was often near disaster. Yet he survived against these great odds and eventually triumphed, due partly to his own military genius and partly to the dissensions among the enemy coalition. The peace of Hubertusburg, which marked the end of the Seven Years War, left Prussia in undisputed possession of Silesia, but a million people had perished. Tiny Prussia was the foremost military power in Northern Europe.

At the time of Frederick's death in 1786 the Prussian standing army numbered over 200,000 men, totalling 110 field and forty-three garrison battalions, and 273 squadrons of cavalry. It cost in maintenance thirteen million thalers out of a revenue of twenty million.

From 1763, until the outbreak of the French Revolution, Prussia enjoyed a period of peace marred only by the mutual suspicion between Berlin and Vienna. Frederick the Great, in order to safeguard himself against being isolated without European allies, concluded a treaty with Russia in 1764. In 1772 he persuaded Catherine the Great to undertake the first partition of Poland and he induced Austria to take a share of the spoils. Prussia's new gains connected Brandenburg territory directly to East Prussia. In 1779 it looked as if Prussia and Austria might go to war again, this time over the Bavarian succession, but

A group of Prussians including a Gefreiter of 3 Posen Infantry (58), a non-commissioned officer of von Bredow's Dragoons, a trooper of uhlans in undress and a hussar carrying a lance

the difference was patched up by the mediation of Russia and France. On his death in 1786 Frederick left Prussia not only with a military reputation unsurpassed in Europe but also with an enormous increase in its territorial boundaries.

Prussia's Demoralization and Decay

Under Frederick the Great, and under his father Frederick William, the Prussian governmental and military system depended for its function and effectiveness on the will and energy of one man, the monarch. The powers of these autocrats were virtually without limit, and their régimes relied for their efficiency not only on example, discipline, and close control, but also on fear and repression. This was particularly applicable to the brutal methods practised in the army. Serfdom still existed in Prussia at the beginning of the nineteenth century.

With the death of the tyrant Frederick and the accession of a weak and politically short-sighted monarch (Frederick William II, 1786–1797), a reaction set in. Liberalism was in the air and the influence of the Illuminati and the Rosicrucian Society gained ground in the Prussian court and governmental circles. Under this new system all felt free to express themselves, irrespective of their experience or station. Officers interfered in church matters, theologians in political affairs, the diplomatists lectured the generals, while the generals did not feel inhibited in giving expression to recommendations on foreign policy. The result, said one chronicler, was an administration affecting piety, a bureaucratic church and a political army. This political army was to show itself to be of doubtful value.

The outbreak of the Revolutionary Wars in 1792 temporarily allied Prussia with Austria. That year, however, French levies defeated the Prussians at Valmy. Frederick William used this defeat as a justification, the next year, for a further partition of Poland which secured for Prussia Danzig and Thorn. Two years later, under the Treaty of Basle, Prussia withdrew from the war with France, leaving its allies in the lurch and permitting France to dominate West Germany. That same year (1795) Prussia took part in the final partition which obliterated Poland from the map of Europe.

The Prussian Army under Frederick William II had continued to increase in size; by 1797 it numbered over a quarter of a million men, its annual cost being seventeen million thalers against a gross revenue of thirty million. But it had proved no match for the French Revolutionary Armies, partly because of the obsolescence of its equipment and methods but more particularly due to the demoralization and decay in its political and military leadership. In 1803 Frederick William had to submit to the occupation of Hanover, contrary to the terms of the Treaty of Basle, but he contrived to remain at peace with France until 1806. Then, goaded by the Tsar and smarting under the disputed possession of Hanover, the king found an unusual

Uhlans tracking the course of a balloon (Hulton)

reserve of courage and dispatched an ultimatum to Napoleon, demanding the withdrawal of French troops from Germany. A reply was received within the month in the form of invading French armies which destroyed the Prussian forces at Jena and Auerstädt. At Auerstädt the Prussians were numerically superior in cavalry and artillery and outnumbered the French by two to one. Bonaparte cut Prussia down to size so that it was a shadow of its former self, for it relinquished all its territory west of the Elbe and lost the Duchy of Warsaw to Saxony.

Prussia's Military Reforms

Towards the end of his reign, Frederick William II had set up a commission of military organization which, borrowing from the French Revolutionary Army, recommended the division of the Prussian Army into four army corps, each based on a territorial district, the North Prussian, South Prussian, Silesian and Reserve Corps, the latter being formed from the West German provinces outside Mark Brandenburg.

Although the work of this first commission was inconclusive, the organization was reformed and continued its work under Frederick William's successor, Frederick William III (1797–1840). The commission was instructed in 1803 to make recommendations on the Kneseback and Courbière army reforms which proposed radical changes in the military penal code and the improvement in conditions of the soldier. It was intended also to raise large numbers of national reserve battalions. There was no time, however, to put any of these recommendations into effect before the disastrous defeats of 1806.

In 1806 the regimental organization of the old Prussian Army had differed little from that of Frederick the Great. The 6 and 15 Infantry Regiments still furnished the four battalions of the royal guard; there were fifty-eight line regiments, a Jäger regiment and twenty-four fusilier battalions, in all 234 battalions. The cavalry was little altered from the days of the Great King; thirteen regiments of cuirassiers, fourteen of dragoons and ten of hussars, totalling 255 squadrons. But of this great army of 254,000 men with its 600 field and 430 regimental guns, only 120,000 men ever came into action against the French.

The Paris Convention of 1808 destroyed the old Prussian Army. Henceforth, it was decreed, for a term of ten years Prussia was to limit its standing army to a force of only 42,000 men, made up of 6,000 in the guard, 10 regiments of infantry and 8 regiments of cavalry.

The defeat and the dictation of the Paris Convention acted as the spur for the introduction of the long overdue military reorganization. Side by side with Stein's, Hardenberg's and Humboldt's governmental and social reforms, the abolition of serfdom, a new educational system and a civil service open on merit to all classes of society, Gneisenau and Scharnhorst reformed the army, adhering to the letter of the Paris Convention but not to its spirit. For although the peacetime establishment of 42,000 men was not exceeded, no fewer than forty-four infantry battalions, seventy-six cavalry squadrons and forty-five companies of artillery were included in the total. This regular cadre afforded military training, by the so-called Krümper system, to successive batches of young men, about 20,000 a year, who were called to the colours, rapidly trained, and then dismissed to their homes. By 1813 Prussia could call to arms a force of 250,000 men.

In March 1813, following Napoleon's disastrous campaign in Russia, a royal edict created the Landwehr and the Landsturm, to include all men between the ages of eighteen and forty-five capable of bearing arms.

The Prussian king had been forced into the allied camp by the action of General Yorck, commanding the Prussian contingent of Napoleon's Grand Army, who had gone over to the Russians together with his men. The War of Liberation and the close of the struggle with France found Prussia regenerated with a strong spirit of nationality, and, at the peace of Vienna, Prussia's large army gave it a political importance out of proportion to the extent of its territory or to the numbers of its population. For the final 1815 campaign which ended at Waterloo, Prussia deployed in Belgium four army corps totalling 117,000 men and 300 guns; 83,000 men came into battle at Ligny.

THE PRUSSIAN CONSCRIPT SYSTEM

Prussia had had restored all that it had lost at Tilsit and, in addition, had obtained the grand-duchy of Posen, Swedish Pomerania, the greater part of northern Saxony, the duchies of Westphalia and Berg and the Rhine country between Aachen and Mainz. The new Prussia, in spite of its limited population and finances, was determined to hold its own in the military field by maintaining an army comparable in size with those of the great European powers.

By the law promulgated in 1814, every man was liable for military service from the commencement of his twentieth year, serving three years with the colours and two with the reserve. This component, made up of men up to the age of twenty-five, formed the standing army. After his twenty-fifth year the soldier passed to the rolls of the first section (Aufgebot) of the Landwehr for seven years and then, at the age of thirty-three, to the second section of the Landwehr for another seven years. At the age of forty he could then be transferred to the Landsturm. The Landsturm also included males between the ages of seventeen and forty-nine who had been exempted from regular military service in the standing army and the Landwehr.

The territorial reorganization of the army was put on to a permanent footing (some of it still unchanged in 1939). An army corps of guards and grenadiers and eight corps of the line were formed, the line being assigned to the following provinces: 1st to East Prussia; 2nd to Pomerania; 3rd to Brandenburg; 4th to Prussian Saxony; 5th to Posen and West Prussia; 6th to Silesia; 7th to Westphalia; and 8th to the Rhineland. Each army corps had two infantry divisions of two brigades and a cavalry division also of two brigades. The infantry brigade had two regiments, one full strength line regiment and one cadre regiment of the first section of the Landwehr, which could be rapidly brought up to strength on mobilization.

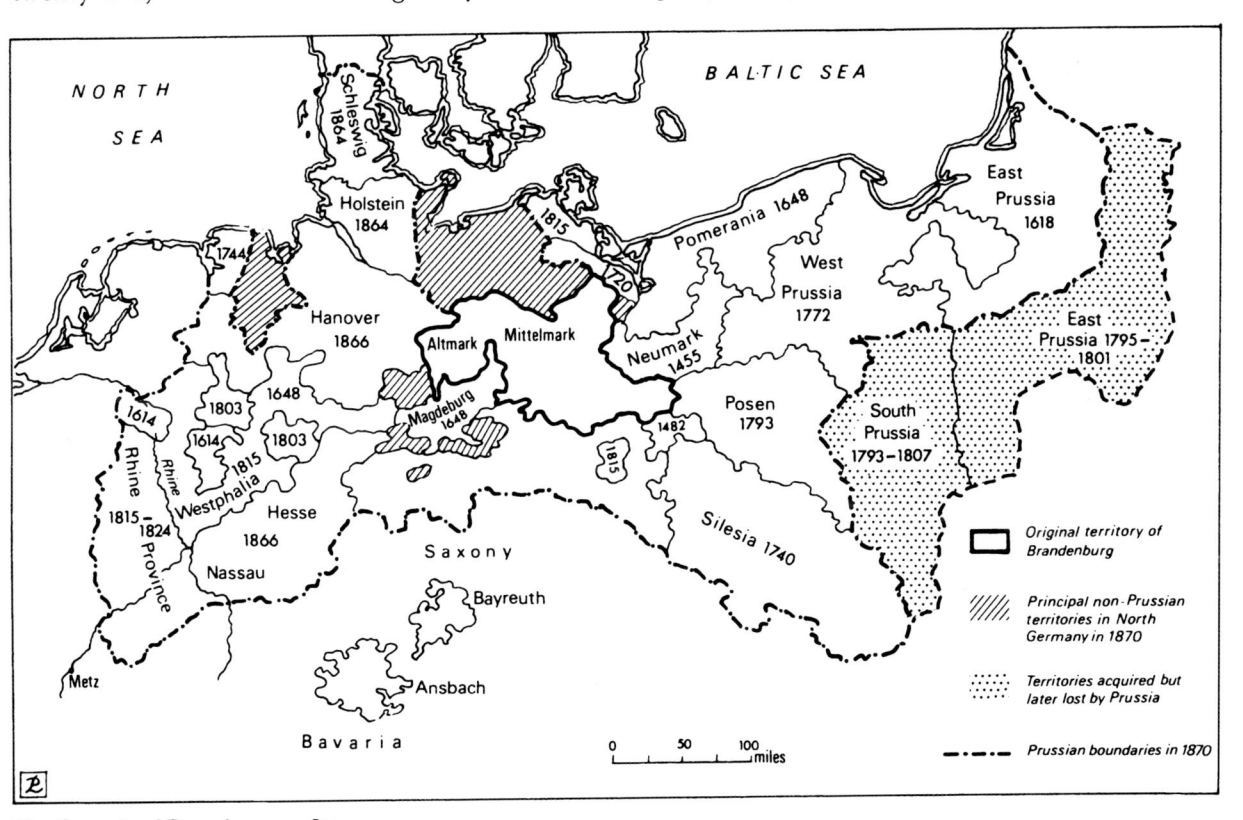

The Growth of Prussia 1400–1870

The cavalry division had two brigades of two regiments, but the four corps troops cavalry regiments were made up of Landwehr. Regiments were permanently garrisoned in, and drew their recruits from, the district surrounding their station. The regular army and the first section of the Landwehr formed the field troops in war, the second section and the recruits providing the immediate reserve. This reorganization was not finally completed until 1830.

Instead of the pre-Napoloenic organization of two battalions to the regiment, the new Prussian Army, together with most other European powers, had introduced the three-battalion regiment both for the standing army and for the reserve. In 1830 the active army stood at four infantry regiments of the guard and grenadiers, thirty-two regiments of line and eight first line reserve infantry regiments, together with thirty-eight regiments of cavalry. The Landwehr consisted of a further forty regiments of infantry and thirty-two of cavalry. The active standing army stood at 130,000 men, but with the embodiment of the Landwehr regiments this total could be doubled. During the long period of peace, until 1859, this organization remained little changed.

Europe in the Mid-nineteenth Century

After the fall of Napoleon the princes of Germany had agreed to unite in a confederation, and a permanent diet of plenipotentiaries from the German states had met at Frankfurt-on-Main under the presidency of Austria. In each state a constitutional government was to be set up, but, although constitutions were in fact granted to many of the smaller states, both Austria and Prussia were opposed to popular representation. Following the French revolution of 1830 there were many disturbances throughout Germany; in some cases these resulted in the grant of a liberal constitution, in other states to repressive measures. In 1834 a customs union (Zollverein) was inaugurated, at Prussian instigation, and this, in addition to removing restrictions on commerce, did much to stimulate the desire for some form of German unity. The third French revolution in 1848 once more found an echo in Germany, disorders breaking out in both Austria and Prussia. Thereafter a more liberal policy prevailed and a national assembly was elected by the German people. This first met in 1848 in Frankfurt, but had a short life of only thirteen months.

Prussia and Austria both made repeated efforts to unite Germany under terms best suited to themselves. Prussia formed what was to become known as the German Union while Vienna did its utmost to reconstitute the confederation. Eventually Prussia consented to the restoration of the constitution of 1815 and from 1850 onwards the diet resumed its sittings at Frankfurt. Prussia's political influence inside Germany was growing steadily, however, both because of the customs union and because Frederick William IV (1840-61) had made Berlin a centre of learning and natural science.

Because of the civil unrest and disorders between Paris and Warsaw, the peace was, at the best, an uneasy one. New national wars were shortly to break out in unexpected quarters, in Italy and Denmark.

In 1864 Austria had entered upon a war with Sardinia and France in Italy but had been beaten in the battles of Magenta and Solferino. At the peace of Villafranca, which followed, Austria gave up most of Lombardy, Italian territories which it had held for generations.

In 1814 Denmark had been forced to exchange Norway for Swedish Pomerania, the latter being taken away the following year in exchange for Lauenburg and the payment of a million thalers. In 1849 the King of Denmark was obliged to modify the absolutist nature of his monarchy and share the power with a Parliament. The mainly German populations of the duchies of Schleswig and Holstein declined, however, to be incorporated into the new style monarchy or to be ruled from Copenhagen, and this led to a series of wars between Denmark and the German states which terminated only in 1864 when Schleswig-Holstein and Lauenburg were ceded to Austria and Prussia. Yet this joint attack upon Denmark in 1863 and 1864 only increased the mutual hostility between Vienna and Berlin, and before a year was out Prussia had determined to bring to a head the question of the leadership of Germany.

Von Roon's New Army

During the long years of peace the Prussian military organization, still based on the 1814 conscription law, had shown itself to be defective. Unlike the state service the officer corps as a whole was averse to admitting to its numbers any of a bourgeois or plebian origin. The standing army was too small to command much respect in Central Europe and the efficiency of the embodied Landwehr regiments, with which each of the active regiments was paired, was relatively poor by the standards of the regular army. The revolutions and disorders in France, Belgium, Poland and in Germany itself, had called for a partial mobilization of the first section of the Landwehr, but the Landwehr itself had seemed tainted and not too trustworthy in the performance of its duties, for it came to the colours tardily and unwillingly. Finally, because the population of Prussia was growing rapidly, the yardstick of a yearly contingent of 40,000 conscripts available in 1814 bore little relationship to the times or to the large numbers of eligible men fit for military service who were not being accepted simply because the active army lacked the organization to deal with them.

Since 1858 Prince William of Prussia had acted as Regent in place of his unbalanced brother, Frederick William IV; a professional soldier, military efficiency was to him an end in itself. That year General von Roon had drawn up a memorandum for the Regent pointing out the defects of the 1814 mobilization laws and the extent of the unreliability of the Landwehr. The confusion and inefficiency of the 1859 mobilization underlined the criticism and Prince William set up a commission under von Roon to examine the problem and prepare new legislation. Then, since there were some objections from the War Minister, General von Bonin, the Regent replaced von Bonin in his office by von Roon.

Von Roon's recommendations, however, were unpopular with liberal opinion and with the parliamentary assembly, the assembly refusing all grants for military expenditure. Prince William summoned von Bismarck as his new minister-president, a ruthless authoritarian, who took the view that in the event of deadlock between the crown and the assembly, the crown was entitled to take such action as it deemed necessary for the welfare of the state and the conduct of all business. In 1863 the assembly was dissolved.

Although without legal sanction the Prussian government did not hesitate to introduce von Roon's recommendations, and it was not until 1867 that it was able to pass a retrospective Bill legalizing the reorganization of the armed forces and the altered terms of service. According to the Roon plan, the armed forces were to consist of the army, the navy and the Landsturm, the Landsturm consisting of able-bodied men liable for service who had not, however, undergone regular full-time service in the army or navy. The army was divided into the standing army and the Landwehr as before, but the Landwehr was to be given a different character and function, since it was to provide no regiments for service alongside the regular army. It was to constitute both a second line reserve of reinforcements and a pool of reserve divisions; these, however, were to be formed on cadres and nuclei from the regular army.

In consequence each regular infantry regiment formed a Landwehr cadre regiment out of men detached from its ranks, and in 1860 these were known as 'combined regiments' with the same number as their parent regiments and were brigaded with them. A few months later these combined regiments were redesignated 3 and 4 Foot Guards, 3 and 4 Guard Grenadiers, and 41 to 72 Infantry Regiments. Third battalions were formed for the guard reserve and for the line reserve regiments (which hitherto had only two battalions), these being known henceforth as fusilier regiments. 1 to 12 Infantry Regiments received the name of grenadiers.

The cavalry were increased simply for forming new regiments out of squadrons detached from the parent units. And so 2 Guard Dragoons, 3 Guard Lancers, four new dragoon regiments (5–8) and four lancer regiments (9–12) came into being. From 1864 onwards the artillery was brigaded, each brigade consisting of two regiments, one of field and horse batteries and one of garrison artillery.

Under the Roon reforms the conscript's service started on 1 January of the year in which the individual completed his twentieth year, and was to last for seven years from the date of joining. Of this seven years only three were served with the colours (unless the conscript was a cavalryman when the term was four years) the remainder being spent with the regular army reserve. After the seven years was completed the soldier passed to the Landwehr lists where his name remained for a further five years, the total liability from the date of call-up being twelve years.

At the time of the outbreak of war with Austria in 1866 the Prussian Army consisted of nine guard and seventy-two line regiments (254 battalions), and eight guard cavalry, eight cuirassier, eight dragoon, twelve hussar and twelve lancer regiments (200 squadrons). There were nine brigades of artillery with 864 guns. The numerical strength of the regular army was 470,000 men; that of the Landwehr reserve pool 130,000.

Denmark the casus belli

King William I and his Chancellor, Bismarck, had emerged successfully from their struggle with the Prussian assembly which had refused to make money available to Roon and the Chief of General Staff, von Moltke, to carry out their work of reorganizing the Prussian Army. Encouraged by Bismarck, nationalism in Prussia and the pan-German movement in Germany were becoming more intense and it needed only a foreign war to cement all differences. The Schleswig-Holstein question was admittedly a complicated one. Holstein was almost wholly German in population and Schleswig partly German and partly Dane. Both duchies had been connected with the Kingdom of Denmark since the fifteenth century by a personal link, the duke of both states happening also to be the King of Denmark. King Frederick VII had no male heir and since Schleswig-Holstein (like Hanover) adhered to the Salic Law, it followed that the Danish successor could no longer continue to rule over the German duchies. The Danes had tried to overcome this objection by the terms of the 1852 Treaty of London which recognized the claims to Schleswig-Holstein of the Danish heir, Prince Christian. This agreement was ignored by Bismarck and the German diet, Bismarck backing the counter-claims of Christian's rival, Prince Frederick of Augustenberg.

Bismarck asked for Austria's help which was readily forthcoming, for Austria's military prestige was in decline since Magenta and Solferino. The new war looked easy enough. During the war with Denmark, however, many foreign observers considered that the Austrian troops made a better showing than the Prussian, for the Prussian Army displayed some lack of enterprise, partly owing to the inefficiency and want of judgement of its Commander-in-Chief, von Wrangel.

The war ended in 1864, Prussia holding Schleswig and Austria Holstein as the protecting powers. But no agreement could be reached as to who was the rightful duke, Berlin now changing its tune and denouncing the former pretender, Prince Frederick. Frederick, however, found support in Vienna and so furnished the *casus belli* for yet a second time, but on this occasion for war between Prussia and Austria. Before making a recourse to arms Bismarck isolated Austria from its potential allies by political manoeuvre. Russia and Prussia had an *entente* and a mutual interest in the subjugation of the large Polish population on both sides of their common frontier. Italy could only gain by an Austrian defeat. Britain could be disregarded since its monarch was pro-German and its Prime Minister of only secondary account. The only danger could come from France. So Bismarck hastened to make the journey to the residence of the French Emperor at Biarritz where he misled Napoleon with flattery and vague promises both as to Prussia's ultimate political ambitions and as to his own character. Napoleon afterwards said of the German chancellor 'Ce n'est pas un homme sérieux.'

In 1866 Austria went to war, its principal allies being Saxony and Hanover, and it was defeated in a seven week campaign which ended at Sadowa (Königgratz). The Austrian armies were defeated by the superiority of the Prussian organization and armament, particularly the Dreyse breech-loading needle-gun.

Bismarck refused to annex South Germany, believing that sooner or later it would come voluntarily into the Prussian Empire. He did, however, consolidate Prussia's position in the north by annexing Hanover, Hesse-Cassel, Nassau and other minor states, adding to Prussia a population of 4,200,000. All the states north of the Main now formed the North German Confederation under the leadership of Prussia, the first meeting of its diet taking place in Berlin in February 1867. It was the armies of the North German Confederation which were to defeat the French.

The Army of the North German Confederation

The annexations and the new confederation added three new army corps (9, 10 and 11) to the Prussian lists. The armies of the newly incorporated states (Hanoverian, Hanseatic, Frisian, Hessian, Schleswig, Holstein, Nassau, Mecklenburg, Brunswick and Oldenburg) were partially disbanded, reorganized and reformed, being put on the same organization and establishments as the Prussian. Large numbers of Prussian officers and non-commissioned officers were drafted into these non-Prussian regiments, many of the former officers of the Hanoverian, Cassel and Nassau troops being posted to old Prussian units. In other cases complete Prussian companies formed the nuclei of the new regiments. The new German infantry regiments thus formed took the numbers from 73 to 96 on the Prussian lists. They did not receive their old territorial names until the following year and it was some years before they were stationed again in their old recruiting districts.

As with the infantry, so with the horse. In October 1866, squadrons were given up by the old Prussian regiments to form the basis of new cavalry, eight additional regiments of dragoons (9 to 16), East Prussian, Brandenburg, Pomeranian, Kurmark and Silesian in addition to Hanoverian and Schleswig-Holstein, five hussar regiments (13 to 17), Hanoverian, Hessian, Schleswig-Holstein and Brunswick, and four regiments of lancers, Hanoverian, Schleswig-Holstein and Altmark. In 1867 all Prussian cavalry were

Officer aspirants of 1 Leib-Grenadier-Regiment No. 100 (Degen and Portépeé Fähnriche)

11

ordered to form a fifth squadron which would form a reception and depot unit in war and so hasten the process of mobilization. That same year the Mecklenburg and Oldenburg cavalry were incorporated into the Prussian as 17, 18 and 19 Dragoons.

In the artillery additional 9, 10 and 11 Regiments were formed in the same manner as the infantry regiments, the Mecklenburg batteries forming 9 while the Brunswick and Oldenburg artillery formed 10 Regiment. Each of these regiments had three field Abtheilungen of four batteries (two heavy and two light) and one of horse artillery of three batteries.

Other than the annexed Hanover, Saxony was the only large state to be included in the North German Confederation, its troops forming 12 Prussian Army Corps. In 1867 its troops, still under the orders of the Saxon War Ministry, were reorganized on the Prussian model. The sixteen line battalions were formed into eight regiments, to each of which a third battalion was added, and these took precedence on the Prussian lists from 100 to 107, the rifle battalions forming Regiment No. 108. The four Saxon cavalry regiments were added to the Prussian lists as 18 and 19 Hussars and 17 and 18 Lancers. The Saxon cavalry artillery, engineers and train retained its own distinctive uniform, but the infantry gave up its green tunic with blue trousers and adopted the Prussian dress.

The whole army of the North German Confederation was armed with the needle-gun, and its artillery with rifled breech-loading guns on the Wahrendorf system.

Prussia's South German Allies

Bavaria, Württemberg, Baden and Hesse-Darmstadt, all allies of Prussia outside the North German Confederation, maintained their own armed forces.

The Bavarian Army was comparatively large, for it included one regiment of the guard and fifteen of the line, three cuirassier, six light horse and three lancer regiments, four regiments of artillery and a regiment of engineers. By a law of 1868 the Bavarian military establishments were rationalized on the Prussian model; infantry battalions were reduced from six to four companies and a cuirassier and lancer regiment were broken up to raise the remaining cavalry regiments to five squadrons, each of 125 men. The artillery and engineers were reorganized partly on the Prussian design. Although the artillery totalled over 200 rifled breech-loader guns the general service rifle used by all arms was the old Podewil converted breech-loader. Even by 1870 only four rifle battalions had been equipped with the improved Werder rifle.

In Württemberg and Baden the military establishments were somewhat modest, fifteen infantry battalions and ten cavalry squadrons for one, and thirteen battalions and twelve squadrons for the other. The Prussian field guns and the Dreyse

An uhlan Gefreiter and two private soldiers from 2 Magdeburg Infantry Regiment

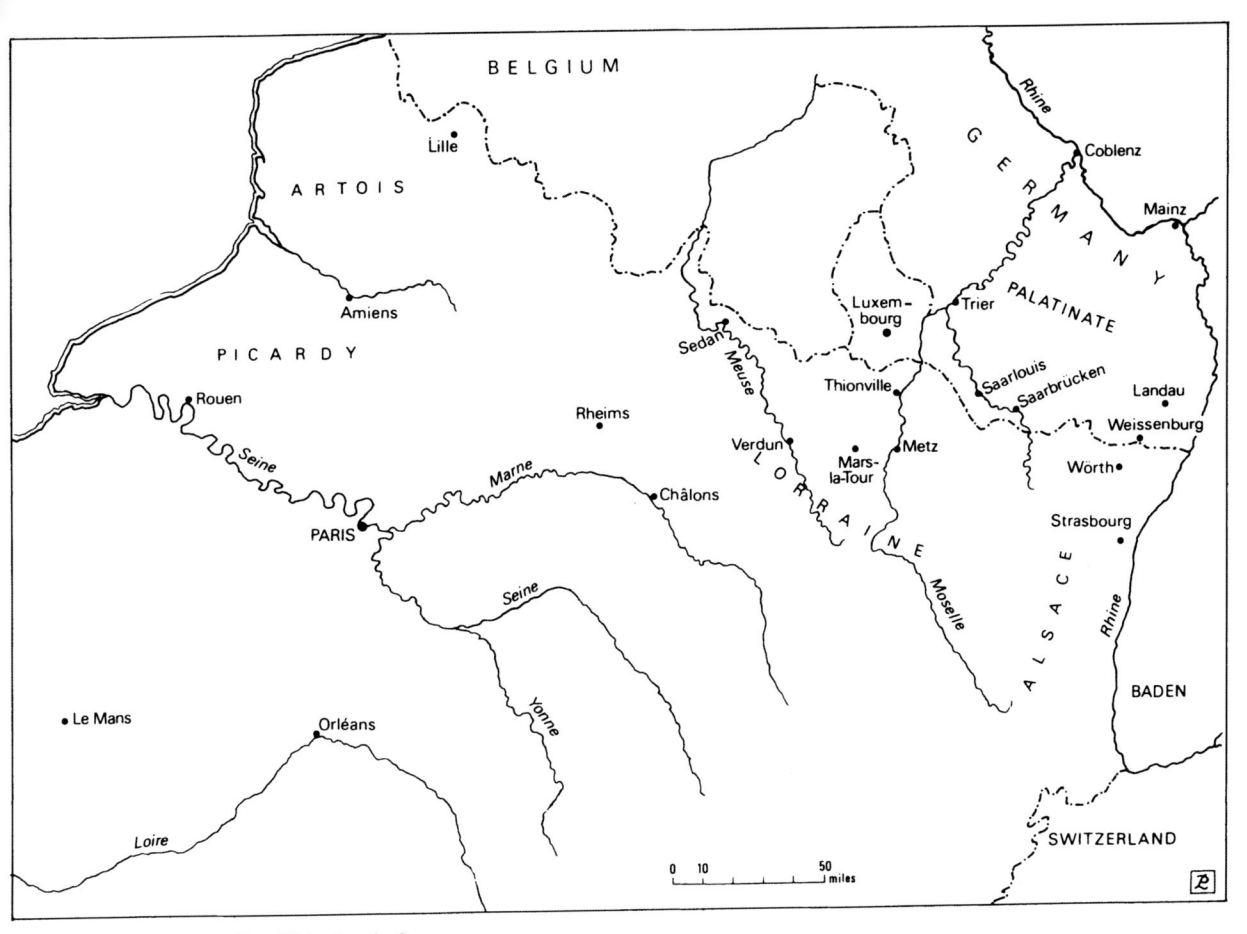

Northern France and The Rhineland 1870–71

needle-gun rifle had been taken into use and Prussian army institutions and drill introduced. The troops of Hesse-Darmstadt, by a special convention, formed the 25th Division of the North German Army.

By 1870 the strength of the German field army was as follows:

	Infantry	Cavalry	All Arms (including garrisons and depots)
North German Confederation	385,000	48,000	982,000
Bavaria	50,000	6,000	129,000
Württemberg	15,000	1,500	37,000
Baden	12,000	1,800	35,000
Total	462,000	57,300	1,183,000

Throughout North Germany there was a wave of national patriotism, much of it fed by the press. Yet the enthusiasm for the war or for Prussia was by no means general. In Hanover and in the Rhineland there were many who would have delighted in a French victory. In Bavaria and Württemberg neither the burghers nor the army was wholehearted in accepting the Prussian leadership. The Prussians for their part had resolved to deal delicately and with tact with Bavarians and Württembergers; the Prussian Crown Prince, who had been appointed Commander of the Third Army made up of contingents of South Germans, hastened to call and pay his respects to the kings of Bavaria and Württemberg. But in reality he was much downhearted by the standards of the troops forming his new command and was doubtful how they would fare against the French.

The Franco-Prussian War

Isabella, the Queen of Spain, had been deposed in 1868 and when the Spanish throne was offered to the Duke of Genoa, he refused it. Bismarck contrived to put forward Prince Leopold of Hohenzollern–Sigmaringen, a Roman Catholic relative of the King of Prussia, and it was agreed in July 1870 between Berlin and Madrid that this candidate should be accepted. The French Emperor Napoleon, who had no wish to have a Hohenzollern on both of France's main frontiers, protested to Berlin and persuaded the Prussian king to withdraw his support from his relative. Napoleon and his ministers then became over-pressing and asked King William to undertake that the candidature would never be renewed. It was too much to ask Prussia to bind itself to a course, irrespective of future circumstances, and William, irritated but outwardly calm, informed Benedetti, the French Ambassador, to that effect. The king, who was at Ems, sent a telegram to Bismarck informing him what had happened with a suggestion that the facts might be released to the press.

Bismarck, who was dining with von Roon and von Moltke when the telegram was received, was in favour of war, for Moltke had completed his mobilization and operational plans to cover war with France. Bismarck then published Abeken's sharply-worded telegram, with some editorial omissions to heighten its effect, so that on publication in Paris the impression was given that the French Ambassador had been insulted. French public opinion demanded war. The South German States joined Prussia and Italy remained aloof. In Austria there was still some resentment against France although this was probably outweighed by the general animosity felt towards Prussia. The decisive factor against Austrian intervention, however, was the unrest in Hungary and an unwillingness there to be dragged into German adventures. The Tsar hinted that he would not be averse to taking up arms on Germany's behalf, should Austria interfere. And so Austria remained neutral.

The King of Prussia took the field as the Commander-in-Chief, in spite of his advanced

The advance of the Baden Grenadier Brigade at Nuits, 18 December 1870, from the painting by W. Emele (Hulton)

Franco-Prussian War, 1870-71. Inner detail of Fort Issy II, 1 February 1870 (Hulton)

years, and together with von Moltke, the Chief of General Staff, and von Podbielski, the Generalquartiermeister (Director of Military Operations), set up his General Headquarters in Mainz. In eighteen days of mobilization nearly 1,200,000 troops, both regular and reservist, were embodied and nearly half a million men were moved westwards to the Rhine frontier. The rapid mobilization and concentration was due to good planning and to the efficient use of the excellent German railways; the passivity of the French did nothing to upset the troop concentration, for Paris had impetuously declared war before preparations had been completed. In the French armies confusion reigned.

The main Prussian invasion force consisted of three armies, widely dispersed in the first instance. The right wing was formed by the six-corps-strong Second Army, under Prince Frederick Charles (who had succeeded Wrangel in command at the time of the Danish War); this was advancing from the general area of Mainz towards Saarbrücken; in the centre was the First Army of three corps, under Steinmetz, moving from the lower Moselle at Trier and Wittlich towards Saarlouis; and on the left the Third Army of four corps, under the Crown Prince, moving from Landau into Alsace and Strasbourg. The Third Army was supposed to strike the first blow, while the Second Army in the north completed its longer wheeling approach. For Moltke had hoped to encircle and annihilate the French Army where it stood north of the Saar. But the Prussian army commanders could not make themselves ready in time and Steinmetz was unwilling to submit to Moltke's authority. The Prussians could do no more than win the first two engagements at Weissenburg and Wörth (4 and 6 August) where they defeated Macmahon's I French Corps.

These defeats were by no means serious; the French infantry had fought well while the Prussian performance had left much to be desired.

15

Prussian infantry advancing after Sell, from an illustration in *The Graphic*, 3 March 1870 (Hulton)

Franco-Prussian War, 1870–71. The departure, on 7 October, of M. Gambetta, Minister of the Interior for Tours, in the balloon Armand Barbés (Hulton)

But it brought home in Paris the realization that this war was unlikely to be a repetition of the glorious campaign of 1806 when, within a month, French cavalry were sharpening their sabres on the steps of the Prussian War Ministry. In Paris Olivier's ministry fell and Napoleon was about to give up his post as field commander-in-chief. Bazaine was made the nominal commander of the French Army of the Rhine. Bazaine began to fall back on Metz and, as he withdrew, he was furiously assailed by two corps of the German First Army in an inconclusive engagement which, however, lost the French twelve hours, a loss of time which was to make it impossible for them to withdraw from Metz, even if they had wished to do so. On 16 August the French Emperor at long last took his leave of Bazaine in Metz, advising him to withdraw again without delay to Verdun. Bazaine was now on his own, free from Napoleon's interference.

Bazaine had halted his army of five corps (about 160,000 men) and there the Prussian advance guard, confident that it had to deal with nothing more than French covering forces and rear guards, attacked it in the area of Vionville. Marshal Bazaine was a brave and experienced commander who had risen from the ranks, but he was by nature unfitted for high command. Too often he could not be found, for he spent his waking hours riding round the battlefield attending to trivialities. Throughout the battle of Vionville, he had no idea that he was being attacked by only two German corps. On the Prussian side, Prince Frederick Charles refused to admit until late in the afternoon that he was engaging the bulk of the French field force. Casualties were heavy on both sides. The German cavalry in particular was to regard Vionville as their day of glory. Yet, although the final tactical advantage remained with the French, strategically the battle was disastrous to Bazaine's hopes: the Germans had cut the road to Verdun through Mars-la-Tour.

Bazaine had been given no higher strategic direction and was himself without a plan. He might have been wiser to have attacked. But he neither attacked nor withdrew, but contented himself with fighting a series of delaying actions, as he himself later said, 'to wear the enemy out', so allowing time for a new French force to be assembled about Chalons. At least, that was his excuse. On 18 August another major engagement was fought near Gravelotte, this time against the German First Army which was repulsed with heavy losses; many German troops gave way to panic. Bazaine did nothing to develop a counter-offensive and, morally exhausted, had lost control over his subordinates. The German Second Army came into action alongside the First, and with better success. Yet the issue was in doubt until 19 August when Bazaine ordered a further withdrawal into Metz. There he was to stay.

THE ARMY OF CHALONS AND SEDAN

Near Chalons, Macmahon was forming a new army, made up of 130,000 men and 400 guns. Three corps had been in action before with the Army of the Rhine and others were newly arrived or in process of formation. It was an army that was still in no condition to take the field. Napoleon, who was present with it, could not make up his mind what to do, whether to fall back westwards to cover Paris or to strike eastwards to join the encircled Bazaine.

Meanwhile the German forces had been reorganized. Three corps of the Second Army were removed and became the Army of the Meuse under the Crown Prince of Saxony. This army was to advance to the Meuse in pursuit of Macmahon. The remaining four corps of the Second Army were to remain encircling Metz, with the First Army under its command. Prince Frederick Charles commanded the Metz siege and Steinmetz shortly afterwards lost command of Third Army.

Macmahon had left Chalons and was falling back towards Rheims. Von Moltke was uncertain of the French intentions, but assumed that Macmahon was going to withdraw westwards to cover Paris; eventually, however, by reading the Paris newspapers it became obvious to him that the Army of Chalons was making a circuitous march to the north and west in order to join up with Bazaine in Metz. Macmahon was totally ignorant that the German Army of the Meuse was not about Metz but already making its way westwards. On 31 August the German Third

Four views of the surrender of Napoleon III after Sedan. Above and above right, at the Chateau Belleue on 2 September 1870; the right-hand picture is by Anton von Werner, as is the one below. Right, below, the meeting between Napoleon and Bismark, from a painting by Wilhelm Camphausen. (Hulton)

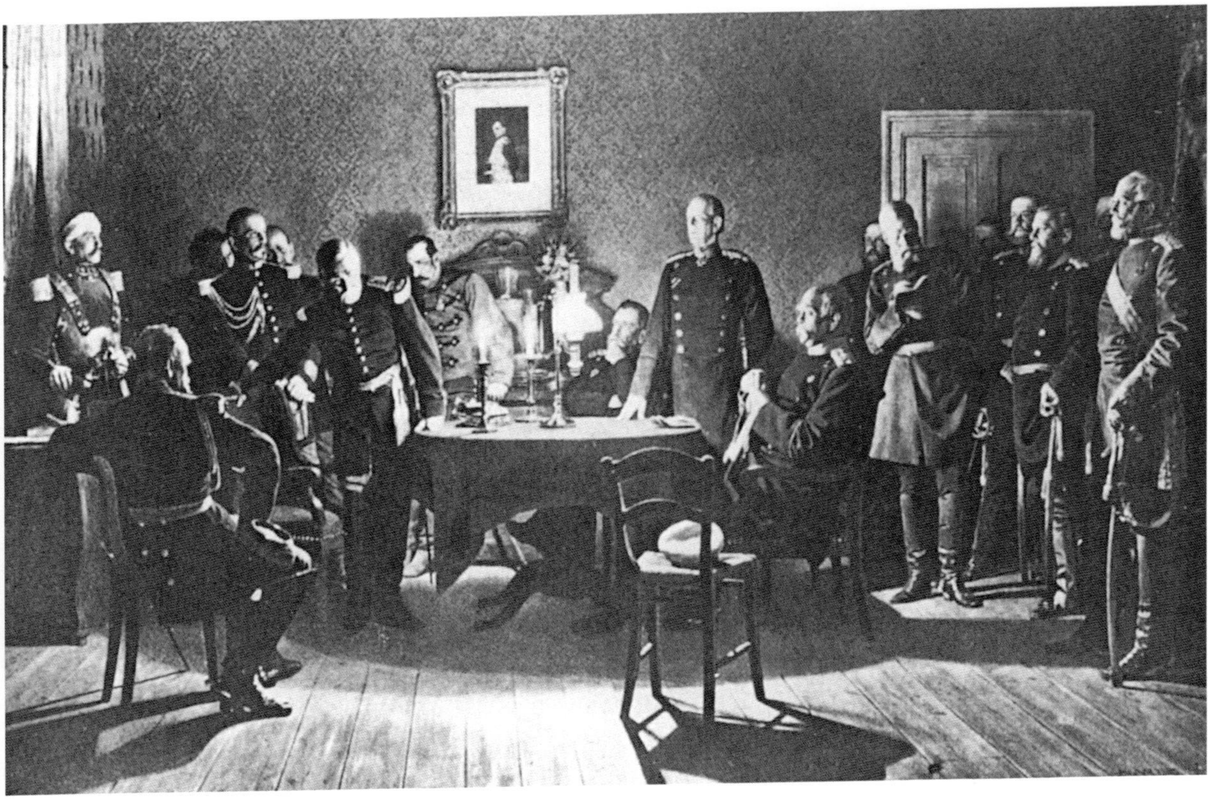

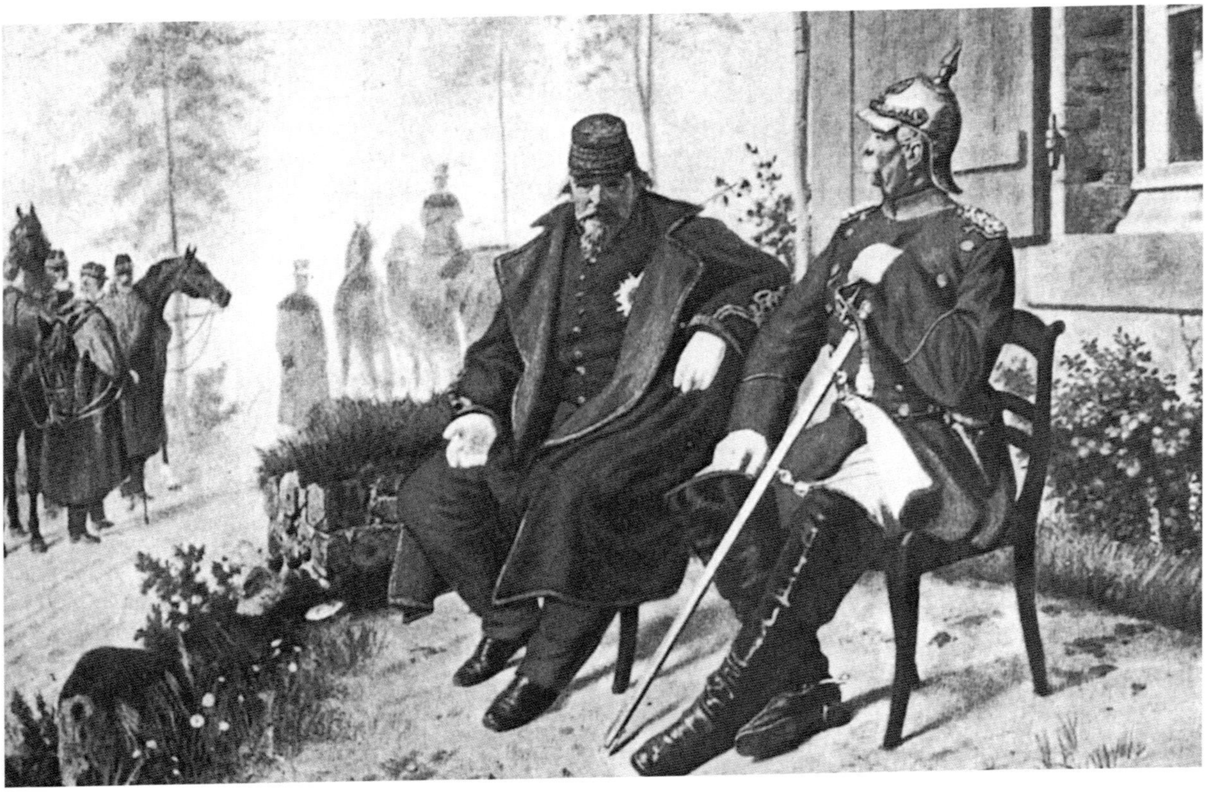

The French guns which were surrendered to the Prussian Army at Sedan. These photographs were taken on 2 September 1870, the day of Napoleon III's surrender (Hulton)

Army and the Army of the Meuse closed up on Macmahon near Sedan, hardly ten miles from the Belgian frontier.

Early next morning 1 Bavarian Corps attacked into Bazeilles which was stoutly defended by French marines and the local inhabitants. Macmahon was wounded early that day and there was confusion as to who should replace him. Ducrot assumed command and ordered a withdrawal to the west to avoid being encircled. Within an hour or so he was replaced by Wimpffen who ordered the troops to stay where they were. Douay's French 7 Corps was the first to break under the heavy weight of the enemy artillery fire between Fleigneux and Floing, and it was followed by 1 Corps which could not withstand the devastating gunnery of the Saxon corps and the Prussian guard. The French began to surrender in large numbers and before evening Napoleon had sent a parlementaire to ask for an armistice. During the battle the Germans had taken over 20,000 prisoners for a loss of about 10,000 men. Except for a number of officers who were released on parole, Napoleon and the whole of Macmahon's army passed into captivity.

So the Second Empire came to an end. For in Paris the news of Sedan led to a revolution; the empress fled and a government of National Defence was set up under Trochu, Favre and Gambetta.

PARIS, METZ AND THE HINTERLAND

On 7 September 1870 the advance on Paris began against unco-ordinated and light resistance, the Army of the Meuse occupying the right bank of the Marne and the Seine, the Third Army the left bank, with their cavalry divisions enveloping the city to the west. By 20 September the operation was complete and Paris was cut off from the outside world. The 150,000 Germans sat down to besiege the capital.

Outside Paris in the hinterland, and indeed throughout France, committees of national defence sprang up in profusion, the resistance movement, at first slow, rapidly growing in momentum. Yet it was very disorganized and often came into existence against the resistance of the French military, who were suspicious of the revolutionary

German troops passing under the Arc de Triomphe, Paris, during the Franco-Prussian War (Hulton)

The entry of Prussian troops into Metz, from *Illustrated London News* of November 1870 (Hulton)

The victorious Prussian occupation army at Fort Issy, 2 January 1871 (Hulton)

Siege of Paris, 1870–71, from the painting by Binet (Hulton)

socialists. Small arms, however, began to arrive from abroad in considerable quantities. Gambetta called on the population to wage a fierce partisan war against the invader, in the first stage harassing and making him thin out his troops before Paris. This was to be a prelude to the resistance taking over more serious operations. The sharpshooting *franc-tireurs* took the field and the war entered a new phase.

Meanwhile Bazaine and the Army of the Rhine sat inactive in Metz. On 26 August the planned movement to join up with Macmahon had been cancelled almost before it had begun. So this great force stood idle until October when it began to run out of rations. On 28 October Marshal Bazaine, without striking a blow, capitulated to an inferior German besieging force.

By the *levée en masse* new French forces had been created on the Loire and this army corps was pressed into immediate action to relieve Paris; it was, however, unfortunate in its first engagement with I Bavarian Corps, which captured the city and depots of Orleans. The *franc-tireurs* were active in the Vosges. And in the north-east in Artois a new French force was being raised. On the other hand, with Bazaine's capitulation at Metz, the two German armies under Prince Frederick Charles had been released for service elsewhere.

The French corps on the Loire attacked the Bavarians at Coulmiers and, after a day's fighting, won the first French victory of the war and retook Orleans. By then the Prussian corps were arriving from Metz and a few weeks later this French corps was overthrown in a series of battles about Orleans. Bourbaki's attempt to carry the war into Germany ended in total failure, and Chanzy's energetic and valiant endeavours about Le Mans could not affect the outcome of the war. Paris, threatened by internal civil insurrection, surrendered and an armistice was signed on 28 January 1871. The peace was concluded at Frankfurt-on-Main in the following May and by its terms France ceded Alsace-Lorraine, Metz and Strasbourg to Germany and had to pay a war indemnity of £200,000,000.

Ten days before the signing of the armistice, on 18 January 1871, the existence of the German Empire had been proclaimed in Versailles, King William of Prussia, by unanimous choice, becoming the first German Emperor. In the previous November Bavaria, Baden and Hesse, and Württemberg had entered the North German Confederation.

Structure of the Army

LAND FORCES

The entire land forces of the new German Empire were formed into a single army at the disposal of the Emperor in peace and war, the expenses, however, being borne by all states of the Confederation. The Commander-in-Chief of the Army of the Confederation could inspect at will any part of the army except that, before making a visit on non-Prussian troops, he was obliged to

An officer and private soldier of the Infantry Regiment von Horn (No. 29)

Prussian lancers bringing in provisions, from *Illustrated London News* of 3 November 1870 (Hulton)

signify his intention to the sovereign of the contingent concerned. Every German soldier was to obey the orders of the Emperor as Commander-in-Chief of the Confederation, except that Bavarian troops were only so bound in war. In fact the dependence, or independence, of the different German states as regards their military systems, depended much on the nature of the conventions already concluded with Prussia.

The German military system in peace was based on a large measure of decentralization to the army corps, each of which formed a little army in itself, commanded by a general officer responsible for its efficiency and preparedness for war, training and recruiting. There were in all nineteen army corps, of which fourteen were composed almost entirely of Prussian troops and were administered by the Prussian War Ministry. Of the others, two corps were Bavarian, one Saxon and one Württemberger.

These nineteen corps totalled 166 regiments of infantry (513 battalions), twenty-one battalions of rifles, ninety-three regiments of cavalry, thirty-seven regiments (364 batteries) of field artillery, nineteen battalions of pioneers, two railway regiments and eighteen train (supply and transport) battalions. The total peace strength stood at 20,000 officers and just under half a million other ranks. On mobilization the army was divided into the field army for active operations in the field, and the garrison army, which remained at home to assist with defence and the maintenance of order, to recruit and replace personnel and equipment losses in the field army.

THE FIELD ARMY

The German Army could deploy several field armies, each made up of four or five army corps together with two or more cavalry divisions as army troops. The army corps had two (sometimes three) infantry divisions, a corps artillery of about

1 Soldier, Imperial Body Guard Gendarmerie (*Leibgendarmerie*), Palace Guard, (gala) dress uniform, c. 1888

2 Non-commissioned Officer, Prussian Palace Guard (*Schlossgarde*) Company, full (gala) dress, c. 1870

3 Trooper, Guard Cuirassier Regiment, full dress uniform, c. 1870

A

Officer, Guard Hussars Regiment, full dress uniform, *c.* 1875

1 Feldwebel, Fusilier Battalion,
  3 Guard Grenadier Regiment (*Königin Elisabeth*),
  parade full dress uniform, *c.* 1875
2 Trooper, 1 Hessian Hussars (No. 13),
  summer parade uniform, *c.* 1870
3 Officer Aspirant (*Portepeé-Fähnrich*)
  1 Saxon Leib Grenadier Regiment (No. 100) *c.* 1880

1 Gefreiter, Uhlan Regiment Hennings von Treffenfeld (*Altmark*) No. 16, summer parade uniform, *c.* 1870
2 Private (*Musketier*), 3 Rhineland Infantry Regiment No. 29, summer field service uniform, *c.* 1887
3 Drummer (*Gefreiter*), 2 Hanseatic Infantry Regiment No. 76, summer field service uniform, *c.* 1871

Non-commissioned officer, 2 Hanoverian Dragoon Regiment No. 16, summer field service uniform, *c.* **1871**

E

1 Chief of Staff (General Staff),
  field uniform, c. 1871
2 Captain, 1 Hussar (*Leibhusaren*) Regiment,
  parade order, c. 1871
3 Rifleman (*Gardeschütz*), Foot Guards,
  summer field service uniform, c. 1871

F

1 Horse-Artilleryman, 12 Royal Saxon Artillery Regiment, summer field service uniform, *c.* 1871
2 Feldwebel, 1 Guards Field Artillery Regiment, summer field service uniform, *c.* 1871
3 Gefreiter, 1 Railway Engineer Regiment, field service uniform, *c.* 1871

G

1 Gefreiter, 3 Royal Bavarian Light Cavalry Regiment (Duke Maximilian's), summer parade uniform, c. 1871
2 Miner, Silesian Pioneer Battalion No. 6, fatigue dress, c. 1880
3 Infantry Officer, undress uniform, c. 1880

six batteries, a rifle battalion and a pioneer company and administrative services. The infantry divisions each had two brigades, each of two regiments, a cavalry and an artillery regiment, together with a pioneer company and bridging train. The cavalry divisions (of which there were nine on the order of battle) each had six cavalry regiments and two horse batteries.

The nineteen corps of the field army were based on the peacetime strength of the standing army; but this total was backed by eighteen reserve divisions to form part of the field army after mobilization. This reserve totalled 315 battalions of infantry and eighteen reserve cavalry regiments, in all 370,000 men, and comprised those soldiers who, having already completed their three years colour service, had passed to the four year period with the reserve. Reserve soldiers were liable to recall for two trainings, neither of which might exceed a period of eight weeks.

On being discharged from the reserve, seven years after the date on which the soldier was originally conscripted, he passed (as we have already said) to the first section of the Landwehr for a further five years. But the military law of the German Empire, unlike the Prussian system immediately before the Franco-Prussian War, had re-introduced the second section of the Landwehr which retained on its lists all former soldiers between the ages of thirty-two and thirty-nine. The Landsturm of the Empire remained the untrained reserve of men (up to their forty-fifth year) who had never served in the army or the navy.

The entire recruiting and recall system was based on the military territorial organization of the Empire, and its efficiency was proved at the time of both the Austrian and the French wars. The army corps districts in Germany were divided into a number of brigade districts, each the responsibility of the officer commanding the regular infantry brigade. The brigade district was divided yet again into a number of Landwehr battalion districts, each the responsibility of a re-employed former regular field officer on half-pay, these officers having a two-fold task; the call-up of the peacetime conscripts and also the maintenance of the lists of all regular reservists and members of the Landwehr. The commanders of regular or reserve divisions did not have any

Charge at Reischoffen, 16 August 1870, from the painting by A. Morot (Hulton)

responsibility for the administration of reservists or for their call-up.

INFANTRY AND RIFLES

Prussian and German infantry had many distinctions in titles, ranks, numbering and in dress which had their origins in custom or tradition. Most infantry regiments had three battalions, although a few of them had four. The Prussian guard and all Bavarian infantry regiments had their own system of numbering. All other German infantry regiments were numbered consecutively from 1 to 139. Prussian regiments from 1–12 and 89, 100, 101, 109, 110, 119 and 123 Regiments were known as grenadier, the non-Prussian regiments being so named because of their earlier connections with regal or ducal houses; 33–40, 73, 80, 86, 90 and 108 Regiments were known as fusiliers; all others were 'infantry' regiments.

The distinctions in designation did not end there, however. In all four-battalion regiments the battalions were numbered simply from 1 to 4 (usually in Roman figures). Of the three-battalion regiments, in 89 Regiment and in 135–138 Regiments, in all fusilier, in all Saxon and Bavarian regiments the regiments were numbered from 1 to 3. But in all other three-battalion regiments, only the two senior were numbered, the third battalion being known as the fusilier battalion. Companies were numbered in normal sequence throughout the regiments from 1 to 12 or 1 to 16 dependent on whether the regiment was on a three or a four battalion organization.

In the Prussian guard, except the guard fusiliers, and in all grenadier battalions, private soldiers were known as grenadiers; in all fusilier regiments and battalions as fusiliers, except in 108 Fusilier Regiment in which they were called sharpshooters (Schützen); in all other infantry battalions private soldiers were known as musketeers, except in 115 Regiment where they were called guardsmen.

The peace strength of a Prussian infantry regiment of three battalions stood at 1,800 men. In war, when the reserve had joined, it was increased to 3,200. The establishment of rifle (Jäger) battalions was the same as that for infantry. Prussian and Saxon rifle battalions continued to be recruited from foresters and forest workers since they were usually tactically employed in advanced or rear guards under circumstances which called for initiative and marksmanship. If a battalion had to be detached a Jäger battalion was usually selected since these were independent tactical units.

The detail of the uniform worn by German infantry was complicated. Prussian, Saxon and Hessian infantry wore dark blue single-breasted tunics; Württembergers wore dark blue double-breasted. Scarlet piping was worn down the front and on the skirts at the rear, except that Saxon troops wore piping round the bottom of the skirts. Collars were usually scarlet with two bars of white lace as a distinction in the Prussian guard, although a number of other regiments wore these bars in white or in yellow. Sleeves might be Swedish or Brandenburg, the colouring varying by regiments. The shoulder-straps and the piping on the patch of the Brandenburg cuffs served to indicate to which army corps the regiment belonged, but in the Prussian guard the shoulder-straps were of different colours for the different regiments. There were numerous other exceptions and differences. Bavarian infantry wore a light blue tunic while 108 Saxon Regiment had dark green. Trousers for all infantry (except the Bavarian which wore light blue) was usually very dark grey, almost black, with scarlet piping. Each infantry battalion and company could be easily identified by the colour of the sword-knot fixed to the bayonet-frog.

There were some variations too in the traditional Prussian type Pickelhaube helmet. The metal spike had a round base, except in Bavaria where it was worn with a cross-shaped bar; moreover, the Bavarian helmet had a bar of metal running down the back. The Prussian guard, 1–12 Prussian Grenadier Regiments and Bavarian infantry wore a peak bound with metal and metal chin-scales instead of a chin-strap (except on service). There were differences, too, between regiments in the design of the eagle on the front of the helmet.

The German infantryman carried a comparatively heavy load. Belt, bayonet, two cartridge pouches in front with a third pouch behind (carrying in all 100 rounds), knapsack, ration bag, mess-tin, greatcoat, haversack, water-bottle and entrenching tool (spade, pick or hatchet). The weight totalled sixty-four pounds (compared with fifty-five pounds carried by the British soldier in those days).

Before 1870 Prussian infantry was armed with the Dreyse (needle-gun) single-shot breech-loading rifle which, although superior to the small arms used by the Danish and Austrian Armies, was certainly no better than the French chassepot. From 1871 onwards this was replaced by the Mauser breech-loader rifle; this was a bolt action rifle which incorporated the Martini breech-block action, the block falling to open the magazine every time the bolt was pulled back and the spent cartridge ejected. The rifle was, however, of very large calibre (·433 inches) and without the bayonet it weighed eleven pounds. The extreme range of the rifle was 3,300 yards and it was sighted up to 1,600 yards; it was effective up to about 1,000 yards. The rifle was carried by all ranks except officers, sergeant-majors, ensigns, bandsmen and drivers.

CAVALRY

Of the ninety-three German cavalry regiments, six came from Saxony, four from Württemberg, ten from Bavaria and the remainder were Prussian. German cavalry was classified as heavy, medium or light, the ten Prussian cuirassier and the two Saxon heavy cavalry regiments alone counting as heavy, the Bavarian so-called heavy cavalry and all lancers counting as medium, and dragoons, hussars and the Bavarian light horse as light cavalry.

The eight regiments of the Prussian guard cavalry took precedence over all other regiments, the guard cavalry being made up of cuirassiers, dragoons, hussars and lancers. These were followed by the two heavy Saxon regiments. Thereafter regiments took precedence, firstly according to type, cuirassiers, dragoons, then hussars, then lancers (uhlans) and finally Bavarian cavalry, and secondly according to number, the number depending on when the regiment had been admitted to the Prussian lists. A Prussian cavalry regiment totalled about 700 officers and men, the regiment having five squadrons in peace and four sabre squadrons in war. The Garde-du-Corps had the troop organization without that of the squadron.

Cuirassier regiments usually wore a white tunic with regimental stripe facings on the collar, down the tunic front and on the Swedish cuffs. The guard wore the usual bars of white lace on each side of the collar and on the cuff. Pantaloons were in white kersey and overalls in dark grey cloth with scarlet piping. In the two guard regiments and 6 Cuirassiers the helmet was of yellow metal, but it was white in all other cuirassier regiments; the helmet came very low behind and curved backwards to cover the nape of the neck, with a square front peak and a metal scale chin-chain. All cuirassier regiments wore the spike, but in the two guard regiments in full dress the spike was replaced with a white metal eagle. The guard wore copper-coloured cuirasses, but other regiments had a cuirass in black iron. When mounted, leather thigh-boots were worn.

The cuirassier carried the straight and heavy three-bar guard broadsword (the Pallasch). It had a thirty-seven-inch blade and weighed just over three pounds. In war all cuirassiers were armed with a revolver, but twenty-five men in the squadron were equipped with the cavalry 1871 Mauser carbine. This weighed only seven pounds but took the same cartridge as the infantry rifle and was sighted up to 1,300 metres.

German dragoons wore the same cut tunic as was worn by Prussian infantry except that the colour was usually light blue. Piping of regimental colour was worn on the Swedish cuffs, on the tunic front and the skirts and sometimes on the shoulder-straps. Pantaloons were of dark blue and overalls of dark grey with scarlet piping. The helmet was of infantry pattern except that the front peak was cut square with metal binding and the chin-scales were of metal. All troopers of dragoons were armed with the 1871 Mauser carbine and the 1852 slightly curved light cavalry sword; this had a three-bar guard and weighed two and a half pounds.

German hussars wore the hussar tunic, the colour varying by regiment, cut rather short with five rows of lace or cord on the chest. The collar and cuffs were of the same colour as the tunic with trimming and, in the case of the guard

Regonville, 18 August 1870, from the painting by A. Morot (Hulton)

hussars, yellow lace. The olivettes on the lace or cord facings were of metal or wood. The dolman-pelisse, worn loosely over the left shoulder suspended by lace or chain, was worn only by the guard and by 3 and 15 Hussars. Pantaloons were usually dark blue. All hussars wore the low busby of sealskin with the coloured bag. In full dress white hanging plumes were worn. The hussars personal arms were the same as those of the dragoons.

Lancers (uhlans) wore a dark blue double-breasted tunic, with piping of the colour of the facings, with pointed Polish cuffs with a button near the point. Bavarian lancers wore dark green tunics, and Saxon light blue. A distinctive feature was the metal epaulette, without fringes, of the same colour as the buttons with an under surface and background of cloth. Two regiments (17 and 18 Lancers) had epaulettes of metal scales; lancers were the only troops to wear epaulettes in peace and in war. Collars, cuffs, turnback and the under surface of the epaulettes were usually of a common regimental colour.

The lance was ten feet long, had an oak shaft about an inch thick and had a four-edged point of forged steel. Lance flags were black and white in Prussian regiments, green and white in Saxon, black and red in Württemberg, and light blue and white in Bavarian regiments. A lancer sword was distinctive in that it had only a single guard; it was light, only two pounds in weight, and was more curved than that of the dragoons. Non-commissioned officers and trumpeters, who did not normally carry lances, were provided with the dragoon sword. Lancers were normally equipped with the cavalry carbine.

There were three patterns of saddlery; the German for the Prussian cuirassiers, Danish for the Bavarian cavalry and Hungarian for all other regiments. The Hungarian saddle was a wooden tree with wooden arches and bars, a leather seat stretched between the arches, two wallets and flaps, with girth and stirrup leathers attached to the bars. On the seat of the saddle was placed a padded cushion, over which went the shabrack and surcingle. The saddle had both crupper and breastplate, and a folded horse-blanket served as the numnah. The German and Bavarian saddles had no padded seat and, in the case of the German saddle, the shabrack was worn under the saddle; separate flaps covered the wallets. The bridle consisted of a snaffle and a straight barred curb with curb-chain, brow-band, nose-band and throat-lash. The carbine was carried with the muzzle in the off wallet, barrel down, stock inclining slightly upwards so as to be level with the rider's hip, and it was secured in that position by a strap from the small of the butt to the pommel of the saddle. The revolver was worn at the rider's waistbelt except by the cuirassiers who carried it in the off saddle-wallet.

FIELD AND SIEGE ARTILLERY

German field artillery comprised thirty-seven regiments, seventeen of which included both horse and field batteries, the remaining twenty regiments having field batteries only. Field regiments were paired into artillery brigades, an artillery brigade being allocated to each army corps. The artillery regiment consisted of three Abtheilungen (battalions), the thirty-seven regiments totalling 110 Abtheilungen in all. The Abtheilung usually had three or four field or horse batteries, the battery having from four to six guns. The peace strength of a battery stood at just over a hundred all ranks, increased in war to about 170 men.

The two main patterns of field gun were 80 mm (78·5 mm) gun for the horse batteries and the 90 mm (88 mm) for the field gunners. Both were breech-loaders formed of steel tube, strengthened for half its length by steel hoops. Both guns were identically grooved. The system of breech closing was by Krupp's single cylindro-prismatic wedge, and obturation was obtained by a Broadwell ring of pure copper, backed by a steel plate in the wedge. The guns could fire double-walled shell, single-walled shrapnel in which the bursting charge was contained in a central tube, and case shot, a tin cylinder loaded with ball. Percussion fuses were used for the common double-walled shell and a graduated time-fuse for the shrapnel. The 90 mm. gun had a range (for shell) of 4,200 metres, the 80 mm. horse artillery gun about 4,000 metres. Gun carriages were the same for both types of gun, being of cast steel on oak wheels shod in iron tyres; limber wheels were interchangeable with those of the gun carriage. First line ammunition scales were 200 rounds a gun with a further sixty rounds in second echelon with the ammunition columns.

In addition to the field artillery regiments, which were equipped almost exclusively with the

Arrest of an ambulance corps, from the painting by E. Delzitte (Hulton)

The market for dog and cat flesh in Paris (Hulton)

80 mm. and 90 mm. gun, there existed a separate branch of the artillery arm known as foot artillery. In peace this consisted of thirty-one battalions each of four companies, twenty-eight of these battalions being paired to form fourteen regiments. A foot artillery company numbered about 150 all ranks.

Foot artillery battalions did not normally include guns on their establishment since they found the crews and gun teams to man the heavier guns of the siege parks. A section of a siege park numbered up to sixty heavy guns and howitzers. Among the siege artillery was the 90 mm. heavy gun which could fire a fifteen-pound shell up to a range of 8,000 yards, the 120 mm. gun which had the same range but fired a thirty-six-pound shell, the short and belted 150 mm. gun and the short 210 mm., which fired a 170 lb. shell to a range of 4,000 metres. The howitzers included the 90 mm., 150 mm. and the 210 mm. Siege artillery was used principally for the destruction of defensive works and for counter-bombardment.

The field artillery uniform was similar to that for infantry, dark blue with very dark grey trousers, black cuffs and black collars with red piping and with scarlet shoulder-straps. Saxon artillery had dark green tunics with a scarlet collar, cuffs and piping. The helmet was of the same pattern as for the infantry except that the spike was replaced by a ball. In full dress, the guard artillery wore white horse-hair plumes, the horse and Saxon artillery black and the Bavarian artillery scarlet plumes. Foot artillery wore the same uniform as the field artillery except that shoulder-straps were white (scarlet in the Saxon foot artillery).

All non-commissioned officers, mounted artillerymen, gunners and drivers wore the artillery mounted pattern sword. Dismounted men had the short artillery sword, a straight cut-and-thrust weapon with a cross hilt and a gutta-percha grip; its blade was only twenty-six inches long. Except for a number of revolvers, artillerymen had no other weapons, carbines being carried only by the dismounted numbers in the ammunition echelons.

Foot artillery, on the other hand, were armed with the infantry rifle and sword-bayonet.

THE BRAIN OF THE ARMY

The German Army prevailed over the French because of the excellence of its war planning and command organization. Much of this was due to the German General Staff which was based principally on the Prussian General Staff.

The Headquarters of the General Staff (known as the Great General Staff) was located in the Königs-Platz in Berlin and operated under the close supervision of the Chief of General Staff and the Director of Military Operations. It was divided in all into nine sections. The principal of these were the First Section – Foreign Armies East, the Second – Germany, the Third – Foreign Armies West, the Fourth – Railways. The

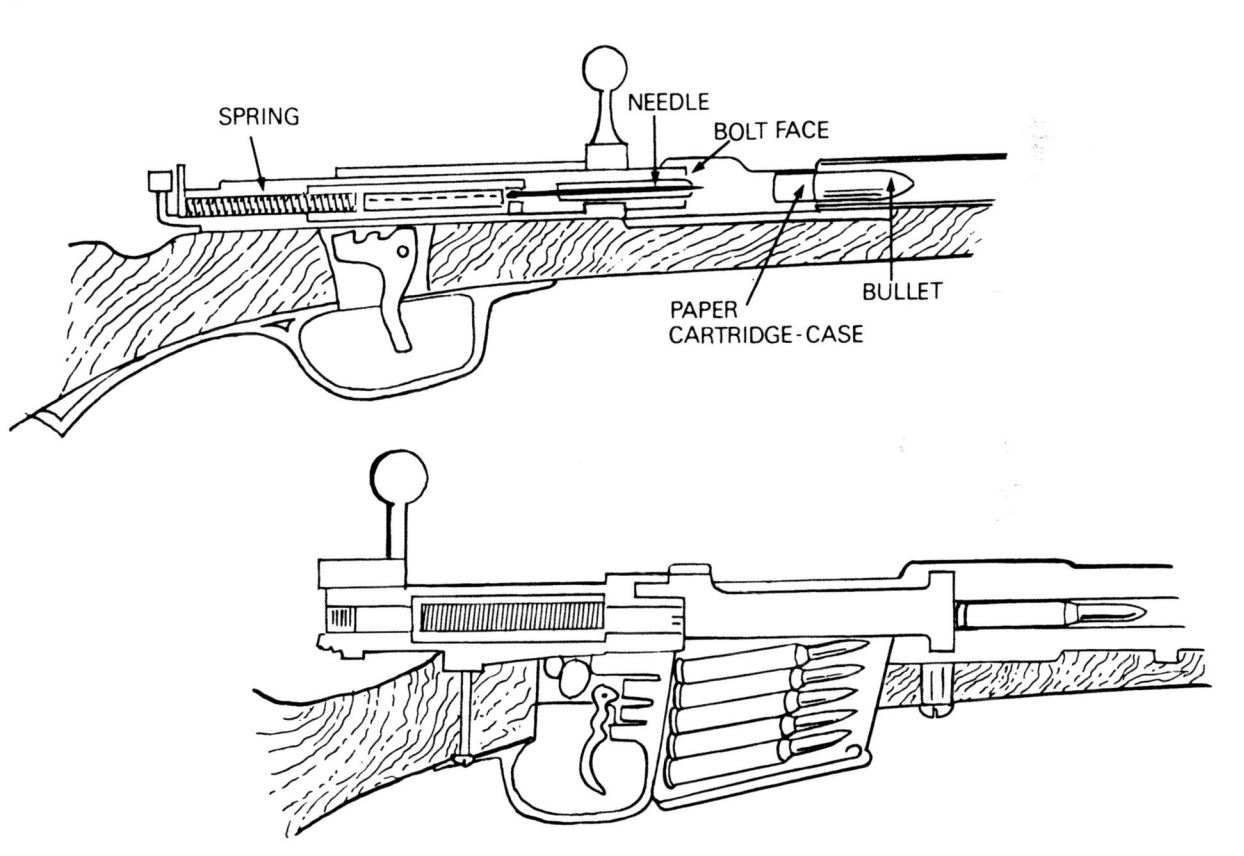

(Above) The Dreyse Needle-Gun of 1841. The bolt closing the breech contained a needle which, on a spring being released, pierced the paper cartridge case striking the detonating composition and igniting the charge. (Below) The Mauser Box Magazine Repeating Rifle, c. 1888. The first Mauser military rifle of 1871 replaced the Dreyse. It had a bolt breech action and in 1884 Germany applied to the rifle a tubular magazine in which the cartridges were carried in a tube in the stock under the barrel. The pattern was changed again to the box magazine shown here. Its rate of fire was superior to the contemporary British Lee-Metford military rifle (which could take ten rounds in its magazine) because of the rapidity with which the magazine could be replenished

remainder covered topography, military history, general intelligence and statistics. In 1887 there were only 167 officers forming the General Staff, but these had status, responsibilities and capabilities far exceeding those normally associated with their rank.

About half of the General Staff officers served in Berlin, the other half being detached to field formations down to the level of divisions. Rarely would more than two officers be allocated to a division and the senior of these would probably be only a major. Yet this officer was responsible for the principal staff work within the division, for advising the commander (who was probably a lieutenant-general or major-general) and for the co-ordination of operations with senior and flanking formations. When the commander was absent, command was automatically assumed by this chief-of-staff or general staff officer, who had a dual loyalty, both to the formation commander and to the separate chain of responsibility of the General Staff. In this way the Chief of General Staff could usually ensure that the spirit of his policy and plans were carried out uniformly throughout the army through the media of the hand-picked and specially trained General Staff. And since General Staff officers in the field had the right, indeed the duty, of direct access to the Great German General Staff, the Chief of General Staff was usually well-informed of the progress of field operations.

Yet the General Staff, and the field formations, depended for their efficiency on the recruiting of suitable staff and regimental officers of all arms. The German corps of officers was regarded by at least one contemporary commentator within the Empire as 'the intellectual and moral aristocracy of the nation'.

Irrespective of arm the officer corps was homogeneous and uniform in its education and training; some were rich, others poor, some were aristocratic and others from the middle-class. But according to the standards of the time all were gentlemen (Hoffähig), all highly educated and

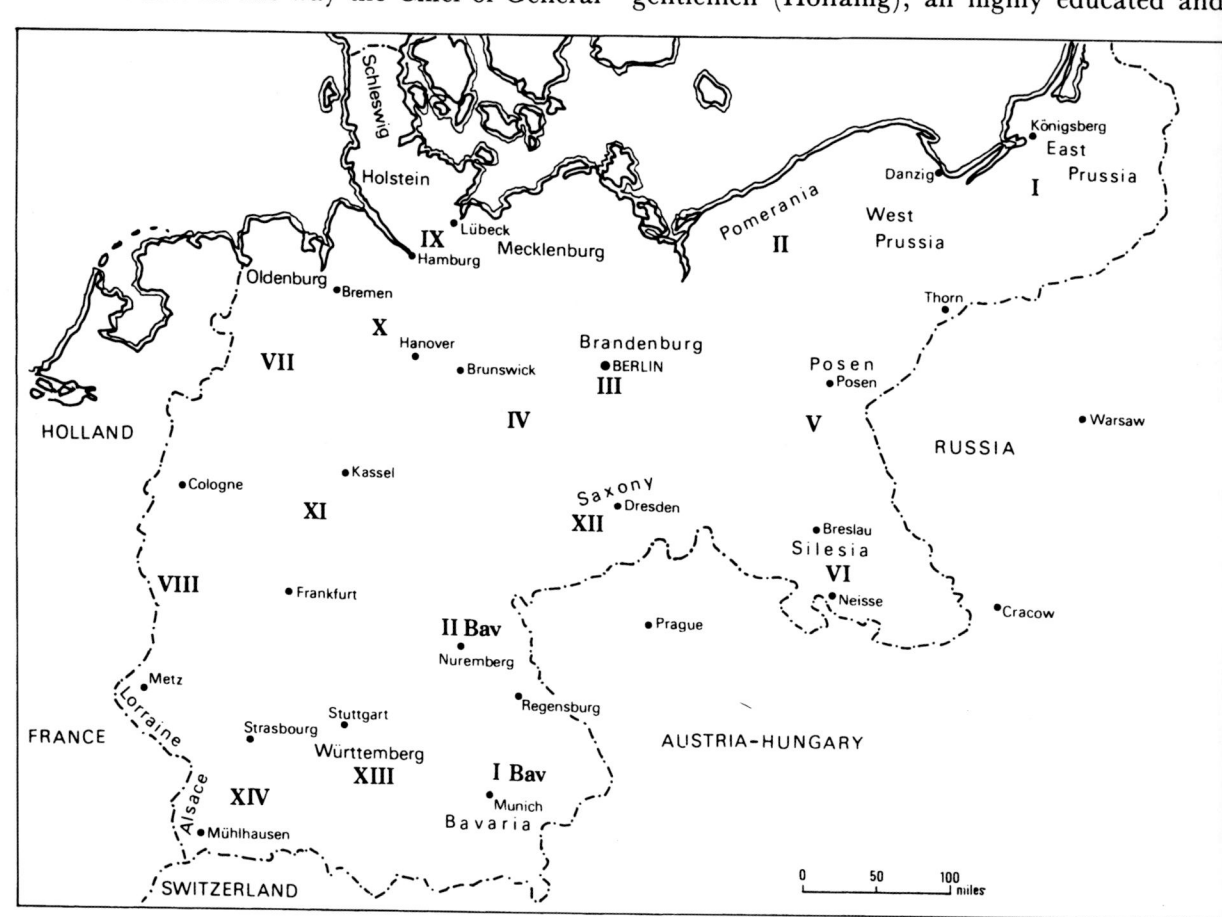

German frontiers and disposition of Army Corps 1887

all were sensitive on the matter of honour, their own personal honour and that of their regiments and of Germany. The monarchs and the aristocracy, almost without exception, served in the army and there could be no greater honour than wearing the 'King's coat'.

Regiments still retained something of a character of a military club in that applicants among aspirant officers had to be approved by the officers of the regiment. This applied also to applicant Landwehr officers who had to be 'chosen' by the officers of their Landwehr battalion district. Yet, in spite of this, sergeant-majors and senior non-commissioned officers who had been discharged from active service with the regular forces, could be appointed as Landwehr officers, presumably to undertake the more technical and routine duties. These commissioned officers who had risen from the ranks were of course quite distinct from the new rank, created in 1877, of Feldwebel-Lieutenant, which was in reality that of a warrant officer, designed to alleviate temporarily the shortage of junior officers.

The pay of the German officer by itself certainly

Engineer officer and soldiers in service, undress and fatigue uniform

did not serve to attract the educated youth to the army. The basic pay for a major-general was the 1870 British equivalent of £37 a month, although substantial subsidiary allowances were added to this; that of a first lieutenant was about £6 a month. No officer could marry without leave and a subaltern officer had to show that his fiancée had a private income of £125 a year; the fiancée of a second-class captain had to have £75 a year. Above that rank no private fortune was required.

Even from the days of the father of the Great King, the German officer had always enjoyed a certain status. But before the wars of 1864, 1866 and 1870, the feeling of the public towards the officers was not effusively friendly. Thereafter officers were received with enthusiasm and pride, forming a class quite apart from the civil population. This in itself was to form a new source of strength to the officer corps. Yet it was to give rise to a governmental as well as a military system which was to admit adventurers and extremists, of whom Bismarck was the first, who were eventually to hasten Germany headlong down its cataclysmic course.

Engineer soldiers of 1 and 2 Railway Regiments and the Engineer Telegraph Company

33

The Plates

A1 Soldier, Imperial Body Guard Gendarmerie (Leibgendarmerie), Palace Guard, (gala) dress uniform, c. 1888

The Body Guard Gendarmerie (the Kaiser's) originally consisted of one officer and twenty-four men detached from Prussian cuirassier regiments for duty in the Emperor's household. The soldiers were retained on the rolls of their regiments and were usually exchanged yearly, the officer in command taking his orders from one of the Emperor's aides-de-camp. In 1889 a second platoon was raised as the Leibwache der Kaiserin und Königin. The uniforms of the platoons were very similar, and both wore the white uniforms shown here as well as another of the same pattern in blue cloth. In addition to posting dismounted guards within the palace, the gendarmerie provided the mounted escorts which accompanied the sovereign's carriage. On those occasions it wore the same uniform as the staff guards of the Garde-du-Corps, a black iron casque with white plumes and aiguillettes, cuirass, cuirassier boots and the cuirassier straight sword (Pallasch). When on duty inside the palace a scarlet cloth imitation cuirass was often worn with the silver star of the guard on the breast and on the back.

A2 Non-commissioned Officer, Prussian Palace Guard (Schlossgarde) Company, Full (gala) dress, c. 1870

In 1829 Frederick William III raised a special company of non-commissioned officers of meritorious service and at least twelve years with the colours who had distinguished themselves in battle; they came from all arms and originally numbered about seventy men, being commanded by an aide-de-camp and by officers (usually convalescents) detached from infantry regiments. The company guarded the royal palaces and gardens in Berlin, Charlottenburg and Potsdam. By 1861 some of these veterans had between fifty and sixty years service and were aged from sixty-one to eighty-three. Since they were hardly fit to undertake further duties they were all pensioned off to make room for a new intake. In 1879 the average age of the company had dropped to forty-seven, with an average of twenty-eight years service between them. The uniform shown here is based on that worn at the time of Frederick the Great and the headdress was somewhat similar to that worn on state occasions by the 1st Foot Guards.

A3 Trooper, Guard Cuirassier Regiment, full dress uniform, c. 1870

In 1807, after the defeat by the French, only two Prussian cuirassier regiments remained, the Garde-du-Corps and Kürassier Regiment von Wagenfeld. The Guard Cuirassier Regiment therefore had a relatively recent origin, being reorganized in 1815 under von Krafft as the Garde Uhlan Regiment from the Guard Cossack Squadron, which was itself formed from Silesian National Cavalry. Not before 1821 was this regiment redesignated as Guard Cuirassier. In 1860 it formed a new fifth squadron which it gave up as a cadre for a resuscitated Garde Uhlan Regiment. The Guard Cuirassiers took precedence next after the Garde-du-Corps, both regiments wearing bars of white lace on either side of the collar and two such bars on each cuff (not visible in the plate because of the gauntlet). When wearing the white everyday tunic the facings were light blue and the buttons white, and the eagle was replaced by a spike on the helmet; the undress tunic was blue with scarlet piping, the collar, cuffs and shoulder-straps being the same as for the everyday uniform. The copper-covered iron back and breastplates shown in this plate were also worn by the Garde-du-Corps. Squadrons could be distinguished by the different colour of the ball above the white tuft of the swordknot, white for the 1st, scarlet for the 2nd (as in this plate), yellow for the 3rd and so forth.

B Officer, Guard Hussars Regiment, full dress uniform, c. 1875

This regiment owed its origin to a composite cavalry company, reformed in 1813 as a regiment from East Prussian volunteers. It took part in the 1813–14 campaigns against the French and in 1815 it was reinforced by amalgamation with other regiments. In 1823 it took up what was to be its permanent station in the capital, its men being housed in Tuchmacherstrasse while the horses were stabled near the Berliner Thor. In 1843, in company with most other hussar regiments, it lost its dolmans for Attilas with five golden or yellow cords, and from 1860 onwards it gave off cadres and squadrons to form new regiments, 2 Guard Dragoon and 9 Dragoon Regiments. It served with distinction during the 1864, 1866 and 1870 wars. In 1888, when the Kaiser became the Colonel of the Regiment, it was renamed the Leibgarde Husaren Regiment, No. 1 Squadron becoming the Leib-Escadron. The dolman pelisse was taken into use again, (being worn only by the Guard and 3 and 15 Hussar Regiments). The star of the guard was worn both on the shabrack and on the brown sealskin busby. Hussars and dragoons carried the 1852 pattern slightly curved light-cavalry sword with a three-bar guard, 3 ft. 4 in. in length and weighing only 2½ lb. (compared with the 3 lb. straight-bladed Pallasch of the cuirassier).

C1 Feldwebel, Fusilier Battalion, 3 Guard Grenadier Regiment (Königin Elisabeth), parade full dress uniform, c. 1875

Of the nine infantry regiments of the Prussian Guard, the 3 Guard Grenadier Regiment was the eighth in seniority. Its origin was recent and relatively undistinguished in that it had become a guard regiment only since 1861 when the Queen Mother became Colonel of the Regiment. Before that time it had been 1 Combined Grenadier Regiment, only re-entering the regular army lists in 1860 from the reserve, where it had been known as 3 Garde Landwehr Stamm Regiment. In 1863 it had been on border duties in Posen and Silesia and saw service in 1866 at Königgratz and Rognitz, and in 1870 at Sedan and elsewhere. Its first commander was von Winterfeld, and its second von Zaluskowski (he was killed at Le Bourget). The two bars of white lace on the collar was distinctive of the Prussian Guard. The 'Brandenburg' cuffs with the three cuff buttons were usually scarlet for most infantry, but in the Prussian Guard Grenadier Regiments, however, the upright part behind the buttons was dark blue as shown in this plate. Of the Prussian Guard, 1 Foot Guards and 1 Grenadiers had white shoulder-straps, 2 Foot Guards and 2 Grenadiers scarlet, 3 Foot Guards, 3 Grenadiers and the Guard Fusiliers yellow (as here), 4 Foot Guards and 4 Grenadiers light blue. The uniform shown in this plate was also used as walking-out undress except that it was worn with a dark-blue glazed peak forage cap with a scarlet band and piping. In full dress the Prussian Guard wore white horse-hair plumes on the helmet except for bandsmen who wore red, and the third (fusilier) battalions who wore black.

C2 Trooper, 1 Hessian Hussars (No. 13), summer parade uniform, c. 1870

After the war of 1866 Prussia annexed further territory in north Germany and absorbed into the Prussian Army by amalgamation with Prussian squadrons two cavalry regiments of the former Hessian (Kurhessisch) forces. These light cavalry became 1 and 2 Hessian Hussars taking the numbers of 13 and 14 in the Prussian lists. They took part in the 1870–71 war before returning to their permanent garrison stations in Hof Geismar, Mainz and Frankfurt. The uniform shown in this plate was of a common pattern for all Prussian hussars, the low busby sealskin head-dress with the scroll '*mit Gott für König und Vaterland*' with scale chin-chains and the addition of hanging white plumes for full dress, and the Attila tunic worn without the pelisse. Men of 14 Hussars, the sister regiment to that shown here, wore the same uniform except that the tunic was in dark blue cloth.

C3 Officer Aspirant (Portepee-Fähnrich) 1 Saxon Leib Grenadier Regiment (No. 100), c. 1880

The Saxon Leib Grenadier Regiment had a long and distinguished history, having been founded in 1663 as the von Lindau Regiment before being amalgamated in 1692 with the Elector of Saxony's Leibgarde zu Fuss. It saw service in Hungary against the Turks in 1695, in the War of the Spanish Succession and the Silesian Wars. In 1756, when Saxony was overrun by Prussia, the regiment was reformed in Hungary as the Regiment Noe de Crousaz. In the French and the Napoleonic Wars it fought both against and with the French, going over to the allies in 1813. In 1866 it fought on the side of Austria against Prussia. Of the larger states Saxony alone was

A non-commissioned officer and men of 2 Royal Bavarian Infantry (the Crown Prince's). Extreme right a Gefreiter of Bavarian Light Horse

included in the North German Confederation of 1867 and its troops were reorganized on the Prussian model, the eight Saxon infantry regiments taking the numbers from 100 to 107. The Colonel in Chief of 100 Regiment was King Albert of Saxony. Aspirants for commission were taken either from the cadet corps or from the ranks (usually as Avantageure or officer candidates) and, after passing an educational test, were appointed Fähnriche. Before the Fähnrich could be commissioned to the lowest officer grade of second-lieutenant he had to pass a military examination and be accepted by a majority of the officers of the regiment which he wished to join.

D1 Gefreiter, Uhlan Regiment Hennings von Treffenfeld (Altmark) No. 16, summer parade uniform, c. 1870

The Uhlan Regiment No. 16 had been raised in 1866 at Salzwedel and Gardelegen by von Paczensky-Tenczin from cadre squadrons transferred from other regiments, 2 (Silesian), 5 (Westphalian), 6 (Thuringian), 7 (Rhineland) Uhlans. In 1870 the regiment was commanded by von der Dollen and the next year George, Prince of Saxony became its Colonel-in-Chief. The regiment saw much action during the Franco-Prussian War, losing nine officers and 174 men in the cavalry attack at Mars-la-Tour. Uhlans (lancers) could be distinguished by the colour of their tunics, dark blue for Prussian and Württemberg, dark green for Bavarian and light blue for Saxon, the regiments differing by the colour of facings, piping and buttons. They wore the Polish pointed cuff with the button and the distinctive shako. The button on each side of the collar showed the soldier to be a junior non-commissioned officer and the grey-blue sword knot (worn also by private soldiers) that he was a lance-corporal and not a corporal (the corporal's swordknot was in national colours). Lancers were the only troops to wear the epaulette with parade and service uniform. The lancer's sword was of the same length (40 inches) as that of the hussars and dragoons but was more curved and lighter, weighing only two pounds. It had only a single bar guard. Trumpeters, sergeants and corporals who did not carry the lance had the heavier dragoon sword.

D2 Private (Musketier), 3 Rhineland Infantry Regiment No. 29, summer field service uniform, c. 1887

This regiment was raised in 1813 from Cleve-Berg troops and in 1817 it was taken into the Prussian army lists as 29 Infantry Regiment, being based on Koblenz, Ehrenbreitstein, Saarlouis and Trier. In 1860 it received its present designation. It served throughout the 1866 and 1870–71 wars and was later (1889) renamed Regiment von Horn. Private soldiers of infantry were known as Grenadiere if in the Prussian Guard or in the first and second battalions of grenadier regiments, as Füsiliere if in fusilier battalions or regiments, Jäger or Schützen if light infantrymen; in nearly all other regiments they were Musketiere. The tunic shown here was of Prussian (and Saxon, Württemberg and Hessian) design, dark blue with scarlet piping down the front and on the skirts at the rear (except that Saxon troops wore piping round the bottom of the skirts). 29 Infantry Regiment was eventually incorporated into 8 Prussian Army Corps and bore the corps insignia, that is to say, a light blue shoulder-strap; the scarlet shoulder-strap (without the piping on the Brandenburg cuff) was the colour of 4 Prussian Army Corps. The colours of the ball and the conical piece above the white tassel or tuft of the bayonet swordknot showed the company and the battalion to which the soldier belonged, all white denoting that the soldier in the plate came from the first company of 1 Battalion. He is armed with the Mauser rifle and the new 1887 leather equipment.

D3 Drummer (Gefreiter), 2 Hanseatic Infantry Regiment No. 76, summer field service uniform, c. 1871

2 Hanseatic Infantry Regiment was raised in Bromberg in 1866 by von Conta on cadres provided by 2, 4, 6 and 8 Pomeranian Grenadiers and the former Hanoverian Leibregiment and was thereafter based on Hamburg and Lübeck; during the Franco-Prussian War it was commanded by von Neumann and then by von Boehn. The white shoulder-straps and the yellow piping on the Brandenburg cuff show that the regiment is part of 9 Prussian Corps; the red and white upper sleeve shoulder-covers denote that the soldier was a bandsman (the drum-major wore an epaulette fringe on the lower edge of the cover) and the button on the collar that the wearer was a corporal. The soldier wears two cockades (not visible in the plate), the black and white Prussian and the red and white Hanse, fixed to the stud fastening the chin-strap.

E Non-commissioned Officer, 2 Hanoverian Dragoon Regiment No. 16, summer field service uniform, c. 1871

The regiment was formed in 1866 by von Salviati from cadre squadrons from the Westphalian and Rhineland Cuirassiers and the Westphalian and Rhineland Dragoons and it saw action at the siege of Metz and the battles of Vionville, Mars-la-Tour, Gravelotte and St. Privat. In 1871 the regiment was based on Ülzen and Lüneburg. The cut of the tunic of dragoons was the same as that of infantry with Swedish cuffs, always light blue (except in the 23 and 24 Dragoons where it was dark green) and single-breasted (except in 25 and 26 Württemberg Dragoon Regiments). The distinction between dragoon regiments was in facings, piping and buttons, and it was unusual for regimental numbers to be shown on the shoulder-straps (as in this plate). The dragoon helmet differed from that of infantry in that the Prussian eagle was of different design, the front peak being cut square; the chin-strap for all ranks was of metal and not leather. Dragoons in the Prussian cavalry no longer fought dismounted as infantry and were normally equipped with the 1871 cavalry carbine, and the light cavalry sword. This plate is of particular interest, however, since it shows dragoons armed with pistols and lances.

F1 Chief of Staff (General Staff), field uniform, c. 1871

Officers of the General Staff were recruited from regimental officers recommended and selected for the course at the War Academy. A number of successful students were then attached for two to three years to the Great General Staff in the Königs-Platz in Berlin at the disposal of the Chief of General Staff and his deputy the Generalquartiermeister. Those officers considered suitable were then transferred to the General Staff where they remained for the rest of their service. About half of the officers of the General Staff served in the Great General Staff in Berlin, the remainder being employed in fortresses and field formations down to the level of division. The chief of staff with the field formations, who might be a major-general or only a major, depending on the size of formation, invariably acted as the commander in the absence of the commanding general. In this way the General Staff acquired great experience and prestige. In addition to the Prussian General Staff there was at this time a Saxon, Württemberg and Bavarian General Staff, although they were limited in numbers; their staff officers were interchangeable with the Prussian. General Staff officers wore a dark blue tunic (light blue in Bavaria) with crimson collar, cuffs, piping and background to the epaulettes. Two bars of silver lace were worn on each side of the collar and on each cuff. The forage cap, frock coat and overalls were as shown in the plate. The normal infantry helmet with silver ornaments was also worn, a white plume being added when in full dress.

(Left) an officer of Hanoverian Hussar Regiment 15 talking with an infantry officer in undress

F2 Captain, 1 Hussar (Leibhusaren) Regiment, parade order, c. 1871

This regiment was one of the oldest in the Prussian Army having been raised in Brandenburg by von Mackerodt in 1741 as 5 Hussar Regiment, 'the Black Hussars', from a cadre squadron taken from 1 Hussars. From 1745 to 1771 the regiment included a Bosnian squadron of lancers which eventually became 9 Hussar Regiment. 5 Regiment was the only hussar regiment to remain intact after 1807 when, ten squadrons strong, it was renamed von Ruesch (its commander from 1744 to 1758). In 1808 it was divided, each of its two battalions (now reduced to four squadrons) becoming 1 and 2 Leibhusaren Regimente, both wearing the Totenkopf and the same pattern uniforms, except that 2 Hussars wore a white bag to the headdress and had black greatcoat patches, forage cap band and shabrack edges, and not scarlet as in 1 Regiment. The scroll on the headdress for all hussar regiments (from 1 to 16) had the inscription '*mit Gott für König und Vaterland*'. The only regiments to wear the Totenkopf were 1 and 2 Hussars and 17 Hussars (formerly Brunswick Hussars in the British service). 17 Hussars bore on their headdress scrolls the battle honours '*Peninsula, Silicien, Waterloo, Mars-la-Tour.*' Officers wore the same pattern uniform as the other ranks except in the cut and quality of materials; where the men wore yellow or white, officers wore gold and silver, with silver sashes instead of white woollen belts. Hussar officers wore no epaulettes but twisted lace shoulder-cords. Company, field and general officers wore shoulder-straps of different width and design, the difference in rank being shown by stars mounted on the strap.

F3 Rifleman (Gardeschütz), Foot Guards, summer field service uniform, c. 1871

There were two rifle (light infantry) battalions in the guard, the Garde-Jäger Battalion and the Garde-Schützen Battalion, a sharpshooter of the latter being shown in this plate. This battalion had a particularly interesting history since it was

An officer of 1 Hussars (Leibhusaren Regiment)

originally Swiss, being raised in 1814 from the men of Neufchatel (Neuenburg), many of whom had previously served in the French service as Berthier's Neufchatel chasseurs. The battalion, which was 400 strong, was recruited both from the principality and from Switzerland and it took the Prussian Jäger uniform, originally with red shoulder-straps, black collar and Brandenburg cuffs. At one time it served as an induction and training unit for the guards before reverting to the light infantry role in which it took the field in the Schleswig-Holstein, Austrian and French Wars. The black glazed shako shown here was common for all Prussian rifles, except that only the two guard battalions wore the guard star; and only the guard wore the two thick bars of lace on the collar. The Gardejäger wore a similar uniform but could be easily distinguished by the red Swedish cuffs. The weapon used by the rifle battalions was the standard pattern Mauser.

G1 Horse-Artilleryman, 12 Royal Saxon Artillery Regiment, summer field service uniform, c. 1871

Saxon artillery wore their own dark green uniform with scarlet facings, with Swedish pattern cuffs in the horse batteries and Brandenburg cuffs in the foot batteries (this latter distinction being common to most German artillery). Saxon horse batteries also wore metal epaulettes, lined with scarlet cloth, like the guard cavalry, as part of their everyday uniform. The shako with the balled crest, rather than the spike, was common to all artillery, except that the one shown here carried the Saxon badge. In full dress, black plumes were added to the helmet. The soldier shown in this plate is a gunner. Non-commissioned rank was indicated by white or yellow lace stripes on and above the cuff and collar and by buttons on the side of the collar.

G2 Feldwebel, 1 Guards Field Artillery Regiment, summer field service uniform, c. 1871

The Prussian guard artillery wore the ball crest instead of the spike with the guard star superimposed on the spreadeagle. In full dress white horse-hair plumes were fitted to the crest. Two bars of yellow or white lace on the cuff and on the collar also denoted that the soldier was from the guard. Non-commissioned officers, trumpeters

A sergeant-major, non-commissioned officer and Gefreiter of 3 Guard Grenadier Regiment

and mounted men wore the uhlan sword with the single bar guard. Dismounted artillerymen wore a short straight sword, just over two feet long in the blade, with a cross hilt and gutta-percha grip.

G3 Gefreiter, 1 Railway Engineer Regiment, field service uniform, c. 1871

Engineer battalions, except for the guard battalion, wore the yellow number of the battalion on the scarlet shoulder-strap, railway regiments having in addition an E (Eisenbahn) and telegraph companies a T. The guard battalion and the railway regiment both wore the distinctive guard insignia, the two bars of white lace on the collar and on the cuff. Like the guard the railway regiment wore black horse-hair plumes in full dress. The arms of the engineer soldier were the rifle carbine, and a sword bayonet with a saw-back edge. An engineer company rank and file carried about 90 spades, 40 picks and 50 axes, one to a man, these being hung in cases on the left side of the pack.

H1 Gefreiter, 3 Royal Bavarian Light Cavalry Regiment (Duke Maximilian's), summer parade uniform, c. 1871

In addition to heavy cavalry and uhlans, Bavaria had six light cavalry regiments. 3 Light Cavalry was originally raised in 1722 by von Minucci as a dragoon regiment, being converted to light cavalry in 1790. In 1799 it was known as 2 Light Cavalry, in 1804 it was redesignated 1 Light Cavalry, but by 1811 it returned to its original number of 3. The regiment had a long history of war having seen action throughout the Silesian Wars, against France from 1792–1800, against Prussia and Russia in 1806–07, against Austria in 1809 and against Russia in 1812. It also took part in the 1866 and 1870 wars. The light horse tunic, all of them dark green, were cut as for the uhlans, distinction being by facings and the colour of the buttons.

H2 Miner, Silesian Pioneer Battalion No. 6, fatigue dress, c. 1880

The new Imperial German Army had nineteen battalions of pioneers, the number of each battalion coinciding with the army corps to which it belonged. Pioneers were trained in sapping and mining, the construction of field and siege works, the building of bridges and the making and repair of roads. Each battalion, which totalled about 600 all ranks, was four companies strong. In war the battalion formed three field companies and a reserve company, together with two divisional and one corps bridging train. The general service forage cap, as shown here, except for officers and senior non-commissioned officers, was without a peak.

H3 Infantry Officer, undress uniform, c. 1880

Prussian (and German) officers were expected to wear uniform at all times, on duty and at leisure. In the first half of the century officers wore the Leibrock tunic stretching almost to the knee, with epaulettes, over which, in winter, was worn the black greatcoat (Überrock) with a red standing collar and turned-back sleeves with red piping. These were eventually replaced by the modern tunic (Waffenrock) and greatcoat (Paletot). The Überrock remained in service, with some modifications, as an off-duty coat. No epaulettes were worn with it (except by uhlans), but shoulder-pieces were displayed. This officer's double-breasted frockcoat was generally the same for all arms, being of the same colour as the tunic (usually black or very dark blue) with a plain collar and piping on the cuffs and sometimes on the skirts. Sword belts were invariably worn under the tunic. Officers of cuirassiers, uhlans and horse artillery wore a dark blue frockcoat, dragoons light blue; hussar officers wore the Spenzer (Spencer) or the Interimsattila.

INDEX

Figures in **bold** refer to illustrations.

Auerstädt, battle of (1806) 6
Austria, war with Prussia 10–11

Baden Army 12–13
Basle, Treaty of (1795) 5
Bazaine, Marshal Achille François 17, 23
Bismarck, Otto von 9, 10, 11, 14, **18**, **19**, 33

Denmark
  war with Prussia and Austria 10
  wars with German states 8–9
Dreyse breech-loading needle-gun 11, 12–13, 27, **31**

Ems telegram 14

Fort Issy **15**, **22**
franc-tireurs 23
Franco-Prussian War (1870–71) 14–23
Frederick I of Prussia 3
Frederick II (the Great) of Prussia 4–5
Frederick VII of Denmark 8, 10
Frederick Charles, Prince 15, 17, 23
Frederick William, Elector of Brandenburg 3
Frederick William I of Prussia 4, 5
Frederick William II of Prussia 5–6
Frederick William III of Prussia 6, 34
Frederick William IV of Prussia 8, 9

Gambetta, Léon Michel **16**, 20, 23
German Imperial Army
  1 Guards Field Artillery Regiment 39, **G2**
  1 Hussar (Leibhusaren) Regiment 38, **38**, **F2**
  1 Railway Engineer Regiment 39, **G3**
  1 Saxon Leib Grenadier Regiment 35–6, **C3**
  2 Hanoverian Dragoon Regiment No. 16 37, **E**
  2 Hanseatic Infantry Regiment No. 76 37, **D3**
  2 Royal Bavarian Infantry **36**
  3 Guard Grenadier Regiment 35, 39, **C1**
  3 Rhineland Infantry Regiment No. 29 36–7, **D2**
  3 Royal Bavarian Light Cavalry Regiment 40, **H1**
  12 Royal Saxon Artillery Regiment 39, **G1**

  artillery 29–31
  cavalry 27–9
  engineers **33**
  Foot Guards 38–9, **F3**
  General Staff 31–2, 37, **F1**
  Guard Hussars Regiment 34–5, **B**
  Hanoverian Hussar Regiment No. 15 **38**
  Hessian Hussars (Regiment No. 13) 35, **C2**
  Imperial Body Guard Gendarmerie 34, **A1**
  infantry 26–7
  Landsturm 25
  Landwehr 25, 33
  Leib-Escadron 35
  officers 33–4, 40, **H3**
  organization 23–4
  Silesian Pioneer Battalion No. 6 40, **H2**
  Uhlan Regiment No. 16 36, **D1**
  uniforms 26
  see also Prussian Army
Germany, unification of 8–9, 10, 11, 23
Gravelotte, battle of (18 August 1870) 17, 37

Hanover, French occupation of 5–6
Hesse-Darmstadt Army 13

Jena, battle of (1806) 6

Leopold of Hohenzollern-Sigmaringen, Prince 14
Ligny, battle of (1815) 7
London, Treaty of (1852) 10

Macmahon, Marie Edmé Patrice Maurice de 15, 17, 20, 23
Mars-la-Tour 17, 36, 37
Mauser Box Magazine Repeating Rifle **31**
Metz 17, 23, **21**

Napoleon Bonaparte 6
Napoleon III of France 11, 14, 17, **18**, **19**, 20
North German Confederation 11, 12–13
Nuits, battle of (18 December 1870) 14

Paris
  entry of German troops into **21**
  siege of (1870-71) 20, **22**, 23, **30**
Paris Convention (1808) 6
Prussia

  war with Austria 10–11
  war with Denmark 10
Prussian Army
  1 Leib-Grenadier Regiment (Regiment No. 100) **11**
  2 Magdeburg Infantry Regiment **12**
  3 Posen Infantry (Regiment No. 58) **4**
  Guard Cuirassier Regiment 34, **A3**
  hussars **4**
  lancers 24
  Landsturm 6, 7, 9
  Landwehr 6, 7, 8, 9–10
  Magdeburg Hussars (Regiment No. 10) **3**
  Palace Guard 34, **A2**
  uhlans **4**, **5**
  under Frederick II 4–5
  under Frederick William I 4
  under Frederick William II 5–6
  under Frederick William III 6
  von Bredow's Dragoons **4**
  von Horn's Regiment (No. 29) **23**
  von Roon's reforms 9–10
  see also German Imperial Army

Regonville, battle of (18 August 1870) **28**
Reischoffen, charge at (16 August 1870) **25**

Sadowa, battle of (1866) 11
Schleswig-Holstein question 8–9, 10
Sedan, battle of (1 September 1870) 20, **20**, **21**
Seven Years War 4
Silesian Wars 4, 35, 40
Spanish Succession, War of the 3, 35
Steinmetz, General 15, 17

Valmy, battle of (1792) 5
Vionville, battle of 17, 37
von Bonin, General 9
von Moltke, Helmuth 10, 14, 17
von Podbielski, General 15
von Roon, General 9–10, 15
von Wrangel, General 10

Waterloo, battle of (1815) 7
Weissenburg, battle of (4 August 1870) 15
William I of Prussia 9, 10, 23
Wörth, battle of (6 August 1870) 15
Württemberg Army 12–13